Dying to Live

"The uncomfortable goodness of this book challenged my cozy relationship with the American dream and inspired me to realign my desires with the call to 'seek first the kingdom of God.'"

—**Pastor Rick Hazelip,** author of *The Knot*

"Margaret's conversational yet poignant words will grip your heart from page one and won't let go. Each chapter contains new insights on common biblical principles that speak to—and convict—your soul. If you're looking for another book on how to keep a nice home, raise godly children, or be a better spouse, you won't find it here. What you will find, though, is a call to urgently become the tangible examples of Jesus the world is crying out for."

—**Michelle S. Lazurek,** multigenre award-winning author of *An Invitation to the Table* and *Righteous and Lost*

"As I read Margaret's book, *Dying to Live,* I was drawn back to a pure, simple, holy, and eager anticipation to stand face-to-face with my Lord and Saviour and hear, 'Well done, my good and faithful servant.' Through her word pictures and real-life examples, I was challenged to examine my heart to test whether my waters (and commitment) ran shallow or deep. Margaret writes with deep conviction and humility on what I feel is a subject the Church needs to be reminded of in this hour—Jesus is coming soon, so we *must* live ready. This book is full of rich insight and will challenge you, even *dare* you, to look at your life with a fresh perspective and will draw you into a deeper walk with God than you've ever had before."

—**Toni Lagaras,** pastor at the River Church, blogger and host of the *Tea with Toni* podcast

Dying to Live

Dying to Live

Letting Go of Earthly Pleasures to Find Eternal Joy

Margaret Jen Burke

LEAFWOOD
PUBLISHERS
an imprint of Abilene Christian University Press

DYING TO LIVE

Letting Go of Earthly Pleasures to Find Eternal Joy

LEAFWOOD
PUBLISHERS
an imprint of Abilene Christian University Press

LIBRARY OF CONGRESS CATALOGING-IN-PUBLICATION DATA
Names: Burke, Margaret Jen, author.
Title: Dying to live : letting go of earthly pleasures to find eternal joy / Margaret Jen Burke.
Description: Abilene, Texas : Leafwood Publishers, [2024]
Identifiers: LCCN 2024007812 | ISBN 9781684260639 | ISBN 9781684260638 (paperback) | ISBN 9781684268566 (ebook)
Subjects: LCSH: Christian life. | Love—Religious aspects—Christianity.
Classification: LCC BV4501.3 .B8733 2024 | DDC 248.4—dc23/eng/20240513
LC record available at https://lccn.loc.gov/2024007812

Cover design by Greg Jackson, Thinkpen Design | Interior text design by Sandy Armstrong

Leafwood Publishers is an imprint of Abilene Christian University Press.

ACU Box 29138 | Abilene, Texas 79699

1-877-816-4455 | www.leafwoodpublishers.com

24 25 26 27 28 29 30 // 7 6 5 4 3 2

For my dad, who has shown me
the American dream is but a smokescreen.

Contents

ONE

The Discipleship Study

When Jesus predicted his death in the New Testament, he also said he would be raised to life again on the third day. But when Jesus was crucified, his disciples became overwhelmed by the reality of his absence and were too distracted by Friday's events to remember that Sunday was coming. They denied knowing him. They deserted him at the cross. They doubted whom he claimed to be.

Each time I read the Gospels, I find myself wishing I could travel back in time—not only to hear Jesus teach but because someone needs to slap some sense into the twelve disciples. Even when Mary Magdalene told them Jesus had, in fact, risen from the dead, they didn't believe her. After living with and learning from the Son of Man, for years, and being told several times about the events that would take place, they simply didn't remember. It's easy to be annoyed by this, isn't it? But you know what? We're stuck on

Saturday too—largely devaluing the future fulfillment of a miracle promise: Jesus's second and final coming. We're just as distracted, deserting, and doubtful.

We also don't like to wait.

In his article "The Psychology of Waiting Lines," David Maister explains the human mindset associated with having to wait.[1] He mentions that if a season of waiting is uncertain or unexplained, it seems longer to us than a season of waiting that is defined and easily understood. Although waiting aimlessly or indefinitely can make us angry, antsy, or afraid, it also makes us weary. It causes us to experience a tiredness that rapidly steers us to distraction. It tricks us into thinking that there are more important, urgent things ahead. It diminishes the value of whatever it is we're waiting for.

Late last spring, my husband, Carson, and I were in our kitchen discussing summer plans. His work schedule had become unusually busy, and he wanted to make sure his calendar matched mine. I mentioned a few dates—our anniversary trip in June, a weekend with his parents for the Fourth of July, a wedding in early August. I unknowingly listed them in order of importance based on their eventual arrival, not bothering to include the small things we also had on the calendar or things that were okay for him to miss. A bit later, while reading a passage from the book of James, I realized I'd spent the better part of twenty-five years making both spontaneous and calculated plans without acknowledging Jesus or his return. If, when comparing calendars with my husband, I had said, "Well, we have an anniversary trip, so-and-so's wedding, and, oh yeah! Jesus might return," he would've laughed it off and told me I wasn't normal—because that's not normal. And if it's not something that's normal to talk about, it's clearly not something normal to anticipate. Does his arrival feel uncertain, nonurgent, because there isn't a specific date or time attached to it? Or have we postured ourselves in a way that diminishes, on a fundamental level, the reality of his return at all?

Has anyone ever critiqued your posture or reminded you to stand up straight with your shoulders back? While this feels old-fashioned, high-societal, and stuffy, good posture is vital to physical health. Simply put, it's how the body maintains balance and flexibility in coordination with the head, hips, and shoulders. If we don't have the natural ability to keep our shoulders back, our chin level, our hips even; or if we've suffered an injury or illness that keep us from doing so, we may experience "joint strain, neck and back pain, and further injury."[2] The way we posture ourselves spiritually—in alignment with the Father, Son, and Holy Spirit— matters just as much, if not more. Life experiences, such as job loss or psychological abuse, or even the way we were raised, have the power to throw our relationship with the Lord out of alignment— making our posture poor and creating space for distraction, disobedience, doubt, desertion, and disbelief. Poor posture, both physically and spiritually, can have fatal consequences.

Jeremiah, after evaluating Judah's love for other gods, wisely commented on the way they had postured themselves: poorly out of alignment with the Lord. "Does a young woman forget her jewelry, or a bride her wedding dress? Yet for years on end my people have forgotten me" (Jer. 2:32 NLT). This is true still today, with you and with me, in our never-ending, shifting, ebbing, and flowing. We wouldn't forget to pack for a vacation, study for an exam, save up for a house, or practice our tennis serve. But we don't seem to remember that Jesus's return also takes a fair amount of preparation. We may have quiet time early in the morning, we may have a few minutes at lunch to recharge our souls, but then we close our Bible and leave Jesus in the kitchen, the breakroom, the front seat of the car. Even our physical posture in these moments can affect us spiritually. If we're meant to pray nonstop, then it must be okay to talk to God while driving, baking, pulling weeds, or falling asleep. Yet, when was the last time you got on your knees to pray? When was the last time you bowed your head low, outstretched your hands, and talked to God—not in passing, but on purpose—in awe, reverence, and wonderment? We're quick to say that we don't physically bow down to idols, but do we even bow to our own creator? Posture matters.

Jesus's return, regardless of what we think, is the most important thing to know and consider about the future. Matthew 24:36 reminds us that no one, not even an angel in heaven, knows the details surrounding his arrival—it will happen when least expected. When he returns to find me, I don't want to be hunched over and distracted. Instead, I hope he finds me standing tall, lifting my head toward heaven (Luke 21:28). Purposely postured.

Jesus illustrates a posture of readiness using the story of the ten bridesmaids in Matthew 25. Traditionally, a Jewish wedding took place in three parts—the engagement, the ceremony, and the marriage. A year after the ceremony, the groom would come back for the bride so the marriage could begin. Almost like a gap year. Don't ask me why. What's even more confusing is the bride and the rest of the wedding party were expected to be there when the groom arrived, although he usually did so unexpectedly. See where this is going? The bridesmaids, in this particular story, just so happened to be asleep when the groom arrived. Upon waking, they didn't have time to fill their lamps. Only those who were already prepared were allowed to attend the marriage festivities.

Another interesting aspect of this story and one that our culture may better identify with is that bridesmaids were usually expected to look their best for the ceremony. In modern times, it's obvious to the wedding guests that each woman spent time preparing herself for the weekend. Her hair and makeup were done professionally. Maybe she even got a spray tan or lost weight, knowing she would have to be in thousands of photos that won't ever go away. This is probably what it will look like when Jesus returns. We might be spray-tanned and gorgeous. We might be down to a size two. We might look amazing in our champagne-colored, strapless, bridesmaid dress. But it will only take a second for us to realize that we spent far too much time preparing for the festivities and not nearly enough time preparing for the arrival of the most important guest.

Even in the days of Noah, people were enjoying parties and weddings, generally doing their own thing, until the very moment they felt the first drop of rain. At that point, it was too late. I don't want our own response to be this delayed, this heedless. His return is not a "future us" problem, nor should we want it to be. It is immeasurable hope for today. Although it sounds somewhat crazy, shouldn't true followers of Christ sincerely look forward to death? Shouldn't there be a tremendous desire to see Jesus face-to-face? Or do we not actually believe that "to die is gain" (Phil. 1:21 AMP)?

If you're dreading his return or quietly wishing it would be a "future us" problem, I understand your thought process. There have been times in my life—like when my son, Riley, was born— that I thought, *Wow, please wait a second, Jesus! I'm really loving life right now.* This mindset can become all-consuming if you are legitimately enjoying yourself, seem to "have it all," or are largely untouched by the evil that runs rampant. In the here and now of temporary happiness, luxury, and success, it's easy to forget how desperately we need Jesus and the joy that awaits us in eternity. I look back on my shallow, limited perspective and feel guilty and embarrassed. How could I ever want anything more than Jesus himself?

I recently spoke with a friend whose heart has forever been hurting. Her words to me were something like this: "I've given the world everything and still, it isn't good enough. The weight is crushing. There's nowhere to go, no support. I just want a peaceful heart, but I fear I'll never find one." What a reminder of how badly we want Jesus, how greatly we need him. Even someone with a picture-perfect life can only tread water for so long before they begin to drown. Those of us who were treading water but somehow found our way to a life raft (success, happiness, etc.) often forget that we, too, are still waiting for rescue.

We can't afford to overlook the words of the psalmist: "My entire lifetime is just a moment to you; at best, each of us is but a breath. We are merely moving shadows, and all our busy rushing ends in nothing" (Ps. 39:5–6 NLT). When reading this, how can anything be more important than living for Jesus? What if you were told today that he's coming back tomorrow? You might actually then forget your wedding dress, which just became a lot less important.

Supermarket Sweep was a televised gameshow that originated in the 1960s. Each contestant had one minute and thirty seconds to fill their cart with whatever they chose. The value of the items in the cart at the end of the game determined the winning team. If the contestant had an hour to fill their cart, they might have chosen to comfortably browse instead of immediately grab what mattered—things of value. Even with such short lives, sometimes we comfortably browse, forgetting that we only have so long before the buzzer goes off and we're called home. We can't afford to worry about things that are of little value to heaven. "We must quickly carry out the tasks assigned us by the one who sent us" (John 9:4 NLT).

Several women, including one of Jesus's first followers, Mary Magdalene, found his tomb empty on the third morning, and they were puzzled. It wasn't until the angels appeared that the women "remembered" what Jesus had said (Luke 24:8 NLT). I don't want myself or my family, my neighbors, or my church to have the same reaction. He told his disciples several times that he would return, and he's telling us, too. There's no time to browse—we must remember and do.

As frustrated as I get with the disciples, it's important to note that the crucifixion and the hours following are historically referred to as earth's darkest hour. My annoyance isn't justifiable when I've never experienced anything like that myself. On this side of history, we get to know what happens. The Bible reveals to us the story in its entirety. With a much larger picture, we're able to see and somewhat understand what Jesus was doing by going to the cross. In a sense, we get to sit back and relax because we aren't the ones who had to witness Jesus's horrific death and wonder how the story ends. We simply get to look forward to the triumphant joy of his final return. Even still, when our comfortable lives—and I mean this in the best way possible—reach a deeper, darker place, when a little bit of stress is added in, we also forget what God has promised. Yet, the space of doubt, distraction, and desertion we're standing in is the space where Jesus wants to meet us. And just like he did with the disciples, he'll pick us up, dust us off, and set us on the straight but narrow path toward heaven, so we, too, can be fishers of men.

What It Means to Follow Jesus

Simon and Andrew were fishing in the Sea of Galilee when called by Jesus, and "immediately they left their nets" (Matt. 4:20 AMP). They didn't ask questions, make excuses, or offer suggestions— they simply left it all and followed. How many of us refer to ourselves as followers of Jesus but would hesitate if he called us away from everything we know and all that we have? When we feel God nudging us with his will, the first thing we usually do is panic. We consult our doctor, our therapist, our friends. We look at our budget. We contemplate what will make the most sense for our family. Our natural reaction is to try and fit God's plan into what we've already established, the place we're most comfortable, forgetting that God largely works outside of all that. I wonder what our lives would look like if we truly leaned into our faith and followed Jesus, just as the disciples did, putting our families, our jobs, our livelihood—everything—at his feet to follow him.

Matthew 10:38 (NLT) says, "If you refuse to take up your cross and follow me, you are not worthy of being mine." Essentially, what Jesus is saying here is that we must be fully committed to following him, regardless of the cost. Every piece of our heart, in every season, must completely submit to his purposes. Otherwise, we aren't truly valuable to the kingdom. Originally, when I read this, I thought there's no way we'll ever be valuable to his kingdom anyway—we're sinners. But the disciples, too, were sinners. They were regular people like us who may not have had the gift of prophesy or discerning of spirits. They were people who had their own agendas, power struggles, and emotions. They were people who, in Jesus's absence, easily forgot who and whose they were. Yet, they didn't serve for a season and go back to their corporate jobs. They didn't check the box of short-term missions and call it good. They decided to follow Jesus to the ends of the earth and spent their lives fighting to do so. Most continued to travel and share the gospel until they were eventually killed for their faith.

We All Have to Decide What to Do with Jesus

A few years ago, I came across a post on social media that filled me with joy and wonderment. The author, Sandra Thurman Caporale, addressed God's name—Yahweh—and how scholars believe the letters represent breathing sounds, aspirated consonants: "YH (inhale): WH (exhale). So, a baby's first cry, his first breath, speaks the name of God. A deep sigh calls His name—or a groan or gasp that is too heavy for mere words. Even an atheist would speak His name, unaware that their very breath is giving constant acknowledgment to God."[3] Although his fingerprints are all over us, although his blood courses through our veins, he still gives us the ability to choose, how and when, to follow him. Or to not follow. People will hear the gospel and decide it's not for them. They'll hear the truth and then alter it while speaking the name of God every moment of their existence.

If you're an American, you've most likely heard of Jesus—on the Internet, in your social circle—and once you hear about him, a choice is inevitably made in regard to following him. Even creation testifies of his existence, leaving us without excuse if we choose wrong. "For ever since the creation of the world His invisible attributes, His eternal power and divine nature, have been clearly seen, being understood through His workmanship [all his creation, the wonderful things that He has made], so that they [who fail to believe and trust in Him] are without excuse *and* without defense" (Rom. 1:20 AMP—square brackets in the original). Even *not* choosing is a choice.

Just the synoptic Gospels alone give an endless account of the choices that were made by people who encountered Jesus. Mary chose well (Luke 1:28–38). Simon and Andrew chose well (Matt. 4:18–20). The Roman officer in Capernaum chose well, too (Matt. 8:5–13). As did the father of the sick boy (Mark 9:17–27) and the woman who touched the hem of his garment (Luke 8:43–48). Some, however, had the choice and did not choose well. Jesus's own siblings rejected him (John 7:3–5). The Nazarenes raged against him (Luke 4:14–30). Judas betrayed him (Matt. 26: 14–16). Even Pontius Pilate chose wrong by pushing the decision onto someone else (John 18:28–40).

The parable of the farmer sowing seeds reveals the condition of our heart in how we respond to Jesus (Matt. 13:1–23). Some of the seeds land on a footpath and can't take root. The ground here is much too hard. This is where, even when we recognize him, we reject him. Some of the seeds land on rocky, shallow soil—a place where their roots are exposed and they simply can't survive. This is a place where we recognize him but allow our faith to become lukewarm. Some of the seeds land on thorny, weedy soil, and although they begin to grow, they are choked out by other plants. This is a place where too many things vie for our attention, and we don't pick Jesus. The best soil is rich earth where the seed can take root and reproduce, where people give their lives to Christ and fully commit to him.

Some people hear the gospel and don't necessarily reject it but decide to wait a few more years to get serious about it. They postpone following Jesus because they want to have fun first, they want to be in charge of their lives. They aren't willing to change their ways or move away from sin. But we are called to "choose today whom [we] will serve" (Josh. 24:15 NLT). Not tomorrow or next week. This decision is far too serious to be put off any longer. What have you decided to do with Jesus?

If You Call Yourself a Christian, Do You Fully Trust Him?

Most of our friends from college got married right after graduation, moved back home, and settled down. For some reason, I dreaded this normalcy. I wanted the opportunity to experience unfamiliar places and new people. So, when my husband, Carson, joined the military and we were thrust into a life of constant change, I was ecstatic. I remember telling him, when he became worried about routinely uprooting our family, that I would "follow him anywhere." And truly, I meant it. When he comes home and says we're moving, I pack up and I move—whether the place we're going is exciting or not. I fully trust him. However, when he received his pilot's license, I decided, *Wait a minute. I will not*

*follow you anywhere, especially not to the municipal airport. I hate
small, single-engine airplanes. I hate heights. I hate speed.*

While he's not going to force me to fly with him, it's no secret
he's frustrated by my lack of trust. I wonder if sometimes I make
God feel the same way. I trust him in some things but choose not
to in others. Proverbs 3:5–6 (NLT) says, "Trust in the LORD with
all your heart; do not depend on your own understanding. Seek
his will in all you do." In just these two verses, King Solomon is
telling us how to trust God: completely, unwaveringly, with all of
our heart, in everything. Yet there are things that I've, even subconsciously, made "off-limits" to God.

Last year, we were praying about adopting a child from a
country in East Africa. After reading several travel advisories that
urged US citizens not to visit due to crime, terrorism, kidnapping,
and piracy, among a host of other things, I made up my mind. We
weren't doing it. It would be irrational, irresponsible—an easy way
to get killed. I simply nixed the idea without consulting the Lord.
I let the US Embassy's "Do Not Travel" list have the final say after
a section titled "If you decide to travel to . . ." suggested I draft a
will and discuss funeral wishes with loved ones.

I fully relied on God, but only when I found myself in comfortable, familiar places. I wanted his guidance, but only when I
didn't have real questions. I acknowledged his sovereignty, but
only when things seemed to make sense. It was clear I didn't know
how to trust Jesus because for so long I had only been trusting in
the resources he'd provided.

If You Call Yourself a Christian, Would You Risk Everything?

We once hosted a neighborhood Memorial Day barbecue, and by
the next afternoon, maggots were pouring from the trash can in
our garage. If you know me, you know there's nothing worse. I
was devastated, nauseous, and almost in tears when my neighbor

found me at the curb and offered to help. We spent an hour dis-infecting the can, cleaning out the garage, and dreaming up ways to burn the house to the ground. A friend of mine who had been visiting was walking to her car that night and just couldn't stop laughing. She looked at me and said, "How much would I have to pay you to sit in a bucket of maggots?" In case you're wondering, we *are* still friends, and I didn't set the house, or the trash can, on fire. I've pretty much gotten over the maggot ordeal, although I still believe that sitting in a bucket of them wouldn't be worth the money, no matter how much. I'm gagging, even as I write this— you were canceled for a reason, *Fear Factor*.

Although no one was killed or severely injured while com-peting on *Fear Factor*, contestants willingly participated in "death-defying and stomach-churning stunts" in hopes of winning fifty thousand dollars. When fame and fortune are the prize, when pleasure is the end goal, there's a lot of things people find worth the risk: skydiving, racecar driving, or, in the case of *Fear Factor*, bull riding, eating roadkill (that has maggots!), bungee jumping from a helicopter. These are foolish risks, not faithful ones. There's no way this type of carelessness is pleasing to the Lord. Spending three months in East Africa fostering a child into adoption? A faithful risk. Maybe even an ultimate sacrifice. Our hearts just have to determine if the reward for following Jesus is worth the risk required to do so. Spoiler alert: it always is.

Neil Armstrong risked his life to land on the Moon because he was passionate about space exploration. The reward, to him, far outweighed the risk. If you ask me, traveling through space in a metal tube seems like a foolish risk. While I'm proud that Americans were the first on the Moon, I wouldn't be willing to do it myself. Am I also the type of person who claims to be a Christian but isn't willing to do the work of one? The type of person who mistakes faithful risks for foolish ones?

Do you think the Moon landing still mattered to Neil Armstrong when he stood before Jesus? Does a gold medal still matter to an Olympian? Athletes spend their lives training to compete at the highest level only to win a prize they can't carry into eternity. Why don't we, as Christians, have the same dedication? We're even promised a prize that's eternal. "All athletes are disciplined in their training. They do it to win a prize that will fade away, but we do it for an eternal prize. So I run with purpose in every step" (1 Cor. 9:25–26 NLT). Some people are training for a marathon, fully trusting that the reward of completing those twenty-six miles outweighs the risks, which include but are not limited to cardiac events and kidney damage. Are you going to be the runner who finds it worth the risk? Or are you going to choose to walk instead because the risk seems foolish?

What, to you, is worth the risk—for God? Would you sit in a bucket of maggots? Fly in a single-engine aircraft? Sell everything you own? Quit your job? Drain your bank account? As followers of Christ, we're called to risk everything. Yet, our lives are too neat, too pretty, too normal to suggest that we've risked anything at all. Not a single person in the Bible had an easy time following Jesus. Why does it seem easy for us? Philippians 1:29 (NLT) says, "For you have been given not only the privilege of trusting in Christ but also the privilege of suffering for him." Trusting is a privilege. Risking everything is, too.

The Cost of Really Following

Peter was crucified. Thomas was stabbed. Micaiah was tossed in prison. John the Baptist was beheaded. Stephen was stoned. John was exiled. Matthias was immolated. Just in this short list, we have followers of Jesus who were stoned, speared, beheaded, crucified, imprisoned, banished, and burned alive.[4] But we're shopping for tea towels, enjoying luxury vacations, getting our nails done, and calling ourselves followers of Christ. It would appear we risk very little when we choose to follow him—because in the United States, even our "Christianity" is privileged. We don't have to fight for our faith. We aren't forced to choose between Jesus and prison, the gospel and death. We put scriptures on T-shirts, laptops, and vehicles without fearing for our lives. We attend Christian schools and concerts. We pray in public. And while we're extremely lucky to be able to do this, it makes things comfortable and casual. It blurs the lines of what's important and minimizes not only the risk but the reward.

Even Jesus himself told people who listened to his teachings not to follow him until they were able to "calculate the cost" (Luke 14:28 AMP). He knew that for some the cost would seem too great, simply not worth the highest price: loss of life. Yet, how much higher is the cost of not following?

I've noticed that Christians are excited to walk others along the path to salvation; they are delighted to see them accept Jesus into their heart and be baptized. But is the cost of following Christ ever really considered? Take a look at your own journey of claiming your faith. Were you ever told to weigh the cost, or were you told to simply pray a prayer? Were you told that you'd be rejected by the world, made to suffer, killed for your faith (Matt. 16:24)? Were you told that you'd have to live for the purposes of Jesus only (2 Cor. 5:15)? Were you told that God requires a first place in everything (Col. 1:18) and that you'd have to give up everything (Luke 14:33), including sexual immorality, impurity, greed, and evil desire (Col. 3:5–10)? Were you told that you'd have to obey his commandments to the fullest sense (Matt. 19:16–21), or that you'd be a lamb among wolves (Luke 10:3)? Were you told that, after you follow Christ, you're forbidden to still want the things of earth (Luke 9:62)?

I feel like I already know the answer to these questions. Most likely, you weren't encouraged to weigh the cost, to consider the earthly consequences, before you were encouraged to give your life to Christ. This is because the American church has somehow found a way for the cost largely not to matter. We've chosen the path that is wide, narrowing it ourselves to make it look like the path to heaven. We've created a space where we aren't rejected or killed, a place where we don't have to suffer. We can live for the purposes of Jesus *and* the purpose of pleasure and prosperity. We can choose what we give up and which commands we follow.

In other words, the culture of American Christianity has blinded us to the reality of Christ. We have to stop acting like it's possible to have Jesus and everything else, too. We can't pretend any longer that just because we accept him into our heart, we have the privilege of calling ourselves followers of God. He calls us to a hard but holy place. He calls us to a lifestyle that we refuse because, to us, it looks unstable and ugly. This sets my soul on fire. I can't sit here any longer and affirm that I'm a follower of Christ because, with him, it's all or nothing, and I've yet to give everything. If we are to consider ourselves daughters of the king, followers of Christ, women who love Jesus, we need to lay our lives down next to the scriptures and look at where we went wrong. Or whether we were ever *really* right in the first place.

— *Questions* —

1. "'A time is coming,' says the Lord, 'when I will punish all those who are circumcised in body but not in spirit'" (Jer. 9:25 NLT). I consider myself a follower of Christ, but my life often doesn't reflect that. I gossip, complain, and overspend. Do you feel the same about your own life?

2. Is there anything you're not willing to risk for Jesus? If so, list it here. Revisit later. Wrestle with it. Lay it at his feet.

3. What is something you feel you can learn from the disciples?

Prayer

Jesus, help me to count the cost. Help me consider all that's at stake and then have the faith to choose you anyway. Make me worthy of the calling. Open my heart and my eyes so that I may see your truth and choose it. Bring me out of happiness and into a holy place.

NOTES

[1] David Maister, "The Psychology of Waiting Lines," *David Maister*, 1985, https://davidmaister.com/articles/the-psychology-of-waiting-lines/.

[2] Marjorie Hecht, "The 4 Main Types of Posture," *Healthline*, November 19, 2020, https://www.healthline.com/health/bone-health/the-4-main-types-of-posture.

[3] Sandra Thurman Caporale, "YHWH," New Song Community Church, August 29, 2022, https://churchatnewsong.com/yhwh-sandra-thurman-caporale/.

[4] Ken Curtis, "What Happened to the 12 Disciples and Apostles of Jesus?," Christianity.com, April 2, 2024, https://www.christianity.com/church/church-history/timeline/1-300/whatever-happened-to-the-twelve-apostles-11629558.html.

TWO

Drinking the Kool-Aid, Eating the Fruit

I t's easy to read the creation account and shame Eve for being thoughtless and disobedient, but the poor choices *we* make in the face of temptation are arguably more harmful to us in our own lives, our own less-than-perfect gardens. Why? Because our direct access to the Holy Spirit and God's written Word gives us the unique ability to recognize sin and turn away from it with God's help.

> For the Word of God is *alive and powerful.* It is sharper than the sharpest two-edged sword, cutting between soul and spirit, between joint and marrow. It exposes our innermost thoughts and desires. Nothing in all creation is hidden from God. Everything is naked and exposed before his eyes, and he is the one to whom we are accountable. So then, since we have a great High Priest who has entered heaven, Jesus

the Son of God, *let us hold firmly to what we believe.* This High Priest of ours *understands our weaknesses, for he faced all the same testings we do,* yet he did not sin. So let us come boldly to the throne of our gracious God. There we will receive his mercy, and we will find grace to help us *when we need it most.* (Heb. 4:12–16 NLT—emphasis mine)

Simply put, we aren't good at this. We fail to recognize sin for what it is by choosing to believe that our words and actions are harmless, especially when they don't directly go against the Ten Commandments or our nation's laws.

We like to think of ourselves as good people, and usually, the self-examination stops there. We don't feel the need to continuously approach God's throne to ask for grace, mercy, and guidance or to ask him to expose our hidden faults and errors. As a result, we aren't able to fully realize the extent to which our "innermost thoughts and desires" fall short of the glory of God. Jesus used the parable of the Pharisee and the tax collector to explain this. The tax collector recognized his sin and was genuinely seeking God's mercy. He didn't believe himself to be trustworthy, righteous, or better than he really was. The Pharisee, however, seemed to be bragging about and praying only to himself (Luke 18:10–14). We are told that "whoever humbles himself shall be raised to honor" (Matt. 23:12 AMP). Humble, in this context, means seeing things for what they are.

When we commit to following Jesus, we "[nail] the passions and desires of [our] sinful nature to his cross" (Gal. 5:24 NLT). In order to do that, we must first come to terms with our sins and then choose every day not to pry them off again. Romans 6:6 (NLT) tells us that those who have given their lives to Christ "are no longer slaves to sin." Paul was saying here that we have the ability to step out from under the control of sin. We have what it takes to nail our sins to the cross of Christ and leave them there. Do we really believe this? Do we care? Or are we content with our relationship with sin because it provides comfort, happiness, and success? All of humanity is guilty before God, yet, like the Pharisee, we continue to pretend we're better than we really are.

We obscure and squander the truth that God so lovingly shared with us until it's too bent out of shape to hold but traces of what it once was. We use prayer requests to gossip. We confuse our purpose with our profession. We compare our imperfections to those of others so we can feel better about all that we aren't. We change the gospel to lessen the blow of sin and make our lives more comfortable, believing that it's still acceptable in the Lord's sight.

American Idols

Equally important is the fact that we look at things like our spending habits, screen time, and secular accomplishments without considering what they might be keeping us from. Sure, these things are not always bad, but they are usually a misuse of God's resources.

And when we use God's resources to serve only ourselves, we're really suggesting that what he's given us isn't good enough. We're insinuating, by our actions, that there are more important, urgent things ahead of him and his return. When you look at your life through this kind of lens, you're able to see that although you're sitting at the feet of Jesus, you're practicing idolatry there, too.

When Moses was on Mount Sinai with God, the Israelites grew impatient and resolved to look for freedom and fulfillment elsewhere (Exod. 32:1). They decided to indulge in what felt safe and familiar—the worship of a golden calf. In their season of waiting, they chose to focus not on what God had provided, but on what he hadn't. The Israelites, once obedient and holy, were suddenly lacking spiritual maturity and self-discipline. "They worshiped worthless idols, only to become worthless themselves" (Jer. 2:4 NLT).

We respond somewhat the same way in our own wilderness seasons, which, without trying to seem dramatic, are the length of our whole lives—a temporary middle ground, largely overgrown and uninhabited by godliness, experienced between the Garden of Eden and the new Eden described in the book of Revelation. In this wilderness period, we assume that because we haven't bowed to a golden calf, we don't struggle with idolatry. But in reality, an idol is anything that takes the place of God in our heart or life. It isn't always an object or person—it can be a thought, a dream, or a desire. It's even fair to say that materialism is a form of idolatry.

In my early twenties, I attended church regularly but spent the rest of the week unintentionally using my God-given resources to pursue worldly success, worldly pleasure, and the worldly version of my ideal self. I say "unintentionally" because I'd like to believe that I truly didn't know any better. However, I should also admit that some of it *was* intentional, because although I didn't fully realize the extent of what I was doing, I did realize that there was an overabundance of time, energy, and money being used to try and achieve an easy and enjoyable life. I obsessed over backyard renovations, worried about vacation logistics, and struggled with wine pairings for dinner parties—fully aware that what I spent my time on mattered little to heaven. My posture had shifted. My life no longer reflected the importance of the creator, but the creation.

Did I assume that a genuine, full-scale relationship with Jesus could coexist with a genuine, full-scale relationship with the world? According to Scripture, having both isn't possible. We can gain the whole world but lose our soul (Matt. 16:26). We can store up treasure here or store up treasure in heaven (Matt. 6:19–21). No one can serve two masters (Matt. 6:24). Yet, we've modified the Word of God to fit the space where we're most comfortable, and we've tweaked it to support our decision-making and lifestyle choices. Because although we want to serve the Lord, we want to serve ourselves, too.

"I'm living my best life" is typically what someone says when they're reveling in a notable accomplishment or coveted life experience. But what they might actually be admitting is this: "I'm busy wasting time here by placing a weight on things that aren't preparing me for eternity." Okay, suddenly, I'm not concerned about vacation. I don't care about the appearance of the backyard. I have more important things to think about than what type of wine we'll have with dinner. I want to serve the Lord with every penny, every moment. I want to spend my energy seeking eternal life, the things of heaven. In my preoccupation, I'd largely forgotten this, too.

Eve did not need to become like God, but that's what she chose to pursue. Heaven does not demand of us a perfectly decorated home or manicured lawn. It does not require us to have followers on Instagram or to be the CEO of a Fortune 500 company. But that's what we've bought into. That's the goal to be achieved, because our culture believes that even if it's not all there is, it's just as important as whatever it is we're waiting for. C. S. Lewis once suggested that our desires are too weak: "We are half-hearted creatures, fooling about with drink and sex and ambition when infinite joy is offered us, like an ignorant child who wants to go on making mud pies in a slum because he cannot imagine what is meant by the offer of a holiday at the sea. We are far too easily pleased."[1]

If they haven't already, worldly distractions will become all-consuming and will subtly (if not obviously) pull you away from the whole point of your purpose. Think about your life, your choices, and your habits. Whenever you're offered a convenient and self-serving opportunity, occasion, or object, do you choose to participate without regard for what stands on the other side? If so, you're not only like me, but you're also like Eve, Rachel

(Gen. 29–30), Delilah (Judg. 16:4–21), and countless other biblical women.

Maybe in the past, you've just assumed God doesn't concern himself with trivial things like online shopping or home renovations—but he does, because he's after your heart. And sister, your heart is usually after the things that are outward, not upward. Romans 12:2 (AMP) plainly tell us to "not be conformed to this world." The same verse in The Message version of the Bible says, "Don't become so well-adjusted to your culture that you fit right into it without even thinking." Well, this is awkward. I'm not sure a stranger in the grocery store could tell that I love and live for Jesus. A particular circle of my friends probably can't either. My behavior toward myself and, more importantly, others, doesn't always indicate I'm a follower of Christ—and to put it simply, this isn't acceptable.

If you are sitting here worried and wondering, thinking about how your own life is perceived by friends and strangers, it's probably worth admitting that you've also adapted to the world. You became, at some point, a product of your environment. You "drank the Kool-Aid." The first time I heard this phrase, a friend was talking about a new craft trending on social media. She said that as soon as she saw it, she bought the material, went home, and immediately started the project. She joked that she "drank the Kool-Aid." I didn't understand what she meant until I discovered she'd been influenced to try something and did so without really even thinking about it.

The phrase "drinking the Kool-Aid"[2] has a negative backstory but is currently used to describe when an individual hastily tries a (sometimes) harmless new fad without considering its consequences. This may be because of social media, peer pressure, boredom, or because they're searching for something that can't be found here. The phrase has also become a term for blind obedience. And my Kool-Aid? It's the American dream.

Historically, the American dream has given hope to many people—the chance to provide for their family and experience prosperity, success, and upward social mobility. But there's also a dangerous side to this pursuance. The American dream is ingrained in our culture, so whether we choose to participate or not, society funnels us into the mix at a young age. Before we know it, we, too, have made temporary success and comfort a priority in our lives. We are told, more or less, to pursue our passion, make money doing it, and live life the way we want to.

When Carson and I bought our first home, I wanted it to look chic and well-kept. I had walked through too many *Southern Living* Idea Houses to want anything less. I practically grew up in one of those houses and expected myself to create the same sort of space for my own family. When my son was born and we couldn't find daycare, I fought to keep my job because two salaries are more comfortable than one. I spent two whole years begging Carson for a Volvo—drooling over them in parking lots, waving at them as they drove by. Until one day, because we could finally comfortably afford one, he said yes. I was more stunned than excited. For some reason, my materialistic little heart felt guilty that things had suddenly gone my way. I took a step back and thought, *No. If I'm able to casually purchase a luxury car and choose to do so, I'm misusing the resources God so graciously provided. When I stand before the Lord at the end of my life, I want to be able to tell him that I didn't get the Volvo! Instead, I consistently and joyfully chose to pursue what was eternal.*

Carson and I have laughed about the frivolity of this, but in reality, it poses a significant threat to our souls. Everyone has their own version of a "Volvo," whether it's something you can possess, power you can obtain, or pleasure you can experience. As children of God, we may not be "of" this world, but we sure are focused—sometimes solely—on things that make us feel secure and "happy" here. The scariest thing about living this way? It gives the impression that it's possible to love the Lord and find happiness, comfort, and contentment elsewhere.

The American dream compels us to buy into what makes us happy, not what makes us holy, and some of us will never move past the happy phase to find the holy place God has for us. It's almost like there are definitive stages of the American dream, and we all get dumped off at the same starting point—"not yet satisfied"—with the expectation of, one day, achieving the dream for ourselves. We spend years seeking success and satisfaction—"building" businesses, bank accounts, résumés, and families—until, suddenly, we're able to experience the fruit of a dream fully realized (successful career, comfortable home, reliable car). We exhale. We relax. We enjoy. We tell ourselves, "We're rich!" "We're deserving!" "We made it!"

We consistently forget that the shine will wear off, and once again, we'll be in search of something to satisfy us. This time, however, maybe we'll look beyond the power, the possessions, the pleasure, and we'll wander back to the feet of Jesus. Maybe we'll just happen to realize before it's too late that God never intended for us to live like this. We'll empty out our hearts again and search for more, for better, for heaven.

The chart on the next page represents the "stages" of the American dream. The box furthest to the left, "Not Yet Satisfied," characterizes the years you spend seeking success and satisfaction, the seasons of "building." The middle section, "Satisfied," corresponds to the years you spend relaxing and enjoying. You may have to work in order to maintain your lifestyle, but overall, you're experiencing the fruit of your labor. The box on the right, "No Longer Satisfied," represents the years you spend seeking

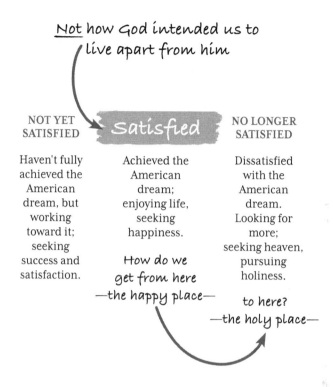

Not how God intended us to
live apart from him

NOT YET SATISFIED	Satisfied	NO LONGER SATISFIED
Haven't fully achieved the American dream, but working toward it; seeking success and satisfaction.	Achieved the American dream; enjoying life, seeking happiness.	Dissatisfied with the American dream. Looking for more; seeking heaven, pursuing holiness.

How do we
get from here
—the happy place—

to here?
—the holy place—

heaven. You aren't as satisfied with the American dream as you'd hoped to be, and while you might still own two houses, a boat, and a Volvo, you're now in search of something better, something more: holiness.

But there will be some people, even those who profess to be Christian, who will spend their whole lives living in this middle space, this season of satisfaction, having fit God's plans and promises into their schedules, their habits, their goals and life dreams. They'll never (re)evaluate their priorities or look beyond the sphere of their own reality. They're too busy succeeding and enjoying life to notice the life and purpose of their creator. The American dream tells us that we can "have it all" if we want it all that bad. But when we stand before God at the end of our lives, he won't look at our résumé. He won't care about our net worth, social status, or education level.

While trying to build my own version of the American dream, I visited Nairobi, Kenya, as part of a short-term missions team. It took roughly twenty-four hours for me to realize that while the locals might benefit from our resources, they don't benefit from our poor imitation of Christ—they don't need Jesus like we do. The week turned out to be less of a mission trip and more of a learning experience as it put both my nationality and love for the Lord in its rightful place. I no longer assumed that because I was from a wealthier, more-educated country that I had a greater purpose in God's eyes or more to bring to his table. I was, for the first time, able to accept the American dream for what it is: a nightmare that not only feels crushing, empty, and unattainable, but also one that keeps us from experiencing true freedom in Christ. From a heavenly perspective, I imagine this dream that is so fundamental to our society is what's suffocating our souls. But because I was young and felt I didn't have a better answer, I chalked it up to experience and continued to drink the Kool-Aid.

Years later, I'm just now beginning to understand how "drinking the Kool-Aid" is the modern way we're "eating the fruit." It's our culture's way of doubting God's goodness, excusing away temptation and sin, chasing the wind. The newest trend might seem innocent and miniscule, but if we aren't careful, we'll spend our lives jumping from one "important" thing to the next, and we'll be too distracted to realize that none of it was real or permanent. We must accept that what distracts us from the Lord really does interfere with our faith and inhibits our ability to be an asset to his kingdom. We must realize that living in "satisfaction" is not what Jesus called us to. In fact, biblically, this lifestyle is compared to salt that has lost its flavor and is no longer good. In Matthew 5:13 (NLT), Jesus says, "You are the salt of the earth. But what good is salt if it has lost its flavor? Can you make it salty again? It will be thrown out and trampled underfoot as worthless."

If we know that we'll never be truly satisfied here (Prov. 27:20) because the Lord has planted eternity in the human heart (Eccles. 3:11), if we know there is danger in satisfaction (Hosea 13:6), and if we know this pursuit is like chasing the wind (Eccles. 2:11), then why are we so quick to follow the American dream? Why do we have to move through these stages, landing on "no longer satisfied," before we realize that Jesus is the only thing that matters? What if our limited time on Earth doesn't allow us to fully work through this process? What if, when Jesus returns, we're still in our happy phase, not having yet reached our holy place? There is an urgency here we don't feel, a reality we don't take seriously.

If your heart is desperately chasing something that doesn't have Jesus written all over it, you've found your Kool-Aid. Maybe you set aside your faith in order to become a social media influencer, a beauty queen, a trophy wife. Regardless of what your Kool-Aid looks like, it's worth admitting the world has firmly grasped your heart. Yet even so, there's no need to panic. He knows the extent of your struggle because, throughout his thirty-three years on Earth, he experienced his own share of worldly distractions and temptations. Indeed, Jesus was also tested. When they were in the wilderness, Satan offered Jesus the whole world (Matt. 4:8–10). The whole world? That's significantly more than what we could possibly acquire or hope for in one lifetime. Still, Jesus refused, and he did so without hesitation, knowing the acquisition of all the kingdoms of the world wouldn't be a way to serve God but himself.

He not only knows what we're going through; he's willing to help. That's why, at the table with Jesus, there isn't forbidden fruit or Kool-Aid, but living water. Jesus explains this to us by first explaining it to the woman at the well. He begins by telling her, "Anyone who drinks this water will soon become thirsty again"

(John 4:13 NLT). Although he's referring here to physical thirst, he's also pointing out the finite satisfaction we find in earthly things, the forbidden fruit, the Kool-Aid. It will never be enough. He goes on to promise her that "those who drink the water I give will never be thirsty again" (John 4:14 NLT). He makes it clear to us that the only way we'll ever be truly satisfied—physically or spiritually—is through him.

Christine Caine, founder of A21, talks about living water in one of her podcast episodes titled "Grab a Shovel and Start Digging." She illustrates the message using the story of Isaac found in Genesis 26. The Lord had blessed him with grain, livestock, and servants to the extent that the Philistines became jealous. In their resentment, they filled all of Isaac's wells with garbage, dirt, and debris, stopping the clean water flow. Caine goes on to share, "today, our wells are stopped up with racism, sexism, materialism, greed, envy, etc., and it stops the clean flow of the water of God. Pick up your shovels and start digging!"[3] When the wells of our heart become muddied and toxic, we must be wise enough to dig new ones, to find again the pure, fresh water that flows from his heart. We must be willing to exchange our forbidden fruit and Kool-Aid for the living water that is the Holy Spirit. Only then, when we sit at his table, will it be possible for us to shift our focus from what's earthly to what is eternal.

Even then, worldly things will vie for our attention and affection, and sometimes, they'll get it. That's the nature of sin. But mostly, we'll choose to rely on Jesus, letting him not only quench the shallowest part of our hearts but the deepest pieces of our souls. This will be a daily battle of turning our eyes to heaven, seeking his face, his presence, his purpose for our lives in hopes that "the things of earth will grow strangely dim in the light of his glory and grace."[4]

— *Questions* —

1. Write about a time you feel that you misused a blessing God had provided.

2. "I once thought these things were valuable, but now I consider them worthless" (Phil. 3:7 NLT). Where do you look for happiness and security? What's important to you right now? Why do these things consume your time and occupy your mind? How can you change your heart to put God first?

3. Do you think it's possible to experience the world fully while experiencing Jesus fully? Why or why not?

4. Jot down some lifestyle decisions, if any, you've made based on the promise of secular security, comfort, happiness, success. Jot down some lifestyle decisions, if any, you've made based on God's will for your life, biblical truth, promises of God, etc. Compare, contrast, and ponder.

Prayer

Forgive me, Father, for being too busy pursuing things here to realize that I don't spend enough time pursuing you and the things of heaven. Capture my heart, Lord,

and allow me to lean into you: Word and your spirit.
Thank you for infinite blessings. Please change my heart
so that all I want to do is give them back to you. The
depths of my soul were made to serve. God, please
ensure I don't get in the way of this. Amen.

NOTES

[1]C. S. Lewis, *The Weight of Glory* (New York: Macmillan, 1949), 1–2. Quoted by the C. S. Lewis Institute, "Reflections: Half-Hearted Creatures," October 1, 2008, https://www.cslewisinstitute.org/resources/reflections-november-2008/#:~:text=We%20are%20half%2Dhearted%20creatures,are%20far%20too%20easily%20pleased.

[2]Chris Higgins, "Stop Saying 'Drink the Kool-Aid,'" *The Atlantic*, November 8, 2012, https://www.theatlantic.com/health/archive/2012/11/stop-saying-drink-the-kool-aid/264957/.

[3]Christine Caine, "The Vault Talks: Grab a Shovel and Start Digging," Passion, YouTube video, 55:34, January 6, 2020. https://www.youtube.com/watch?v=0Ai2ukyggLo.

[4]Helen Howarth Lemmel, "Turn Your Eyes upon Jesus," 1922.

THREE

The *Power* of Inconsistency

If your work isn't consistent, your coworkers won't trust your reliability. If you aren't consistent in your training, you'll never run a marathon, you'll never become a doctor, and your dog will never bring back the ball. And if you aren't consistent in your constant pursuit of the Lord, you will never grow in an intimate relationship with him or become an asset to his kingdom. Inconsistency has so much power. It keeps us from so much. And that's just what I learned when God gave me a high school basketball team.

Like other ways God has worked in my life, the opportunity to serve came up unexpectedly but in a way that, in hindsight, was divinely orchestrated. While my husband and I helped the team financially when and how we could, we chose to serve the students and coaches by simply showing up to after-school practices, games, and weekend events. I have never liked or understood the game of basketball, but when I noticed the players didn't have parents or friends attending the games, the team became a priority in our lives. Before I knew it, we were planning our weeknights around basketball. I have always known that God made my heart to serve others in a powerful way. But until that first season, I only knew how to help in the short term—or really, for however long my time, finances, and comfort allowed. I had written checks, cooked meals, and said prayers, but I had never faithfully considered the responsibility we have as Christians to walk alongside others in the long term. The definition of *walk* is "to move along on foot: advance by steps."[1] It implies that one is doing so in an unhurried fashion—and as the hands and feet of Jesus, God expects this kind of persistence from us.

In Prayer

"And so I tell you, keep on asking, and you will receive what you ask for. Keep on seeking, and you will find. Keep on knocking, and the door will be opened to you. For everyone who asks, receives. Everyone who seeks, finds. And to everyone who knocks, the door will be opened." (Luke 11:9–10 NLT)

"Never stop praying." (1 Thess. 5:17 NLT)

"Rejoice in our confident hope. Be patient in trouble, and keep on praying." (Rom. 12:12 NLT)

In Faith

"Trust in the LORD with all your heart; do not depend on your own understanding." (Prov. 3:5 NLT)

"We live by faith and not by sight." (2 Cor. 5:7 CEB)

"Let us hold tightly without wavering to the hope we affirm, for God can be trusted to keep his promise." (Heb. 10:23 NLT)

In Pursuit of His People

"Love each other. Just as I have loved you, you should love each other. Your love for one another will prove to the world that you are my disciples." (John 13:34–35 NLT)

"Let's not merely say that we love each other; let us show the truth with our actions. Our actions will show that we belong to the truth, so we will be confident when we stand before God." (1 John 3:18–19 NLT)

"Work at telling others the Good News, and fully carry out the ministry God has given you." (2 Tim. 4:5 NLT)

During our time with the basketball team, God showed me the effectiveness of follow-through and the value of endurance. Suddenly, my heart discovered a new way to serve him, and I felt he would use me in limitless ways. We were willing to help the players in whatever capacity they needed—an after-school meal, a Bible study, a tutoring session, a ride home. Carson and I even prayed about the possibility of opening our home, helping with college, and paying light and water bills. I wasn't going to let anything in our lives distract us from the team or the way we were getting to invest in the guys. Or at least that's what I thought.

But then, the coach left. The coach who had welcomed us with open arms and given us opportunities to serve in ways that no other public school would have allowed. And when the following season began, it was clear that the new coaches didn't want us. The dynamic of the team was different. The pandemic was changing things. I was newly pregnant. The games were too far away. The games were too late. We made excuses. We became inconsistent to the point where we no longer made the team a priority or showed up at all. And before I knew it, that season of serving was over.

We haven't seen or spoken to any of the players since. And while I thought we were going to be the difference makers in their lives, having vowed to show up for the long haul, we ended up being the same as everyone else. Just two more people with promises unkept. Two more people who loved until it wasn't easy. My heart shatters when I'm reminded of this, when I fall asleep at night praying for the players whose names I can remember and asking God to hold up those whose name only he now knows. Oh, how my inadequacies, even in service, become glaring when I bow at the feet of Jesus.

Here's the kicker: Jesus isn't the only one who shows up in hindsight. Satan does, too. And he sure works well with inconvenience. He revels in distraction. He hopes for inconsistency. He encourages complacency. He feeds on excuses. And from us? That's what he got. For a long time, I dealt with Satan by choosing to focus solely on the end of his story, which, we all know, is eternal damnation and separation from God (Matt. 8:29) and, thankfully, from us. Satan doesn't have the final say. But placing emphasis on the outcome only barred me from acknowledging that, up until the end, Satan does have a say (John 12:31). I had made light of the fact that Satan was after me and that he would go to great lengths to be a tempter and trickster who would pull me away from the promises and purposes of God.

This thought process also made me forget that sometimes Satan disguises himself to look safe, appealing, even holy. Letting this go unchecked jeopardizes not only your earthly life, but your eternal one. He has convinced our Christian culture that God isn't going to give us more than we can handle, that we're the ones who determine what our limit is. And that gives us space to confuse our human emotion with divine guidance. Our humanity doesn't always sit well with the route we must take to fulfill our kingdom purpose. So, when Satan, unbeknownst to us, offers what looks like a better option, one that's less stressful, one we feel more "peace" about, that's the option we tend to choose.

When church leadership reached out and asked if I would speak one Mother's Day, I laughed out loud, screamed, and then called my husband. I had prayed for years about the message that was on my heart. Had God wanted me to write about it? Speak about it? I didn't know how to do either well. When I spoke to the pastor's wife, Jessie, that day, she said something like this: "Margaret, I don't mean this ugly, but you don't cross my mind often outside of church, but when we were looking for a speaker for this service, I thought of you and just know God commanded this." And she was right—when she initially reached out, she had no idea God had called me to do this. He was at work, no doubt. But even then, two days later, I texted her and asked her to find someone else. I was anxious, unprepared, and, ultimately, too self-conscious to think I had something worth sharing. With the pressure off, I instantly felt better. Well-done, Satan.

Less than ten minutes later, Jessie responded to my text and asked if we could talk through it. In that moment, I knew that because neither of us are ones to walk away from a situation that Satan has his hand on, I would be speaking on Mother's Day. Although he doesn't ultimately win, he wins momentarily, and sometimes that feels just as permanent. God used Jessie to usher in a new sense of what it means to wrestle well. You don't say no to God just because you're restless, anxious, or fearful—you say yes and then wrestle with those emotions. And if you do so *well,* you win. You become a vessel that changes the world—an agent in the trade of souls from hell to heaven.

Sometimes things don't go perfectly, but they *go*, and that's what matters. Your idea of "perfect" is not a standard created by God; it is a standard you chase because the world tells you to. I spoke that day and my voice shook. I had issues with the microphone. I got emotional. But it was clear the message God had given me was meant to be shared. I showed up, and that's what mattered. God did the rest, as he always does. Not today, Satan. Or tomorrow. Or really, ever.

Oh, friend. This is encouragement for you (and me both) to continue the wild and wonderful pursuit of what makes you holy—even when it seems complicated or things don't go your way. Even when it makes you feel overwhelmed, uncomfortable, or momentarily unsatisfied. These bumps in the road are not always God steering you away from what you think he has called you to. Sometimes, these obstacles are just the reality of Satan's existence and proof that he *is* at work, even in the seemingly routine, uncomplicated areas of our lives.

Satan does, in fact, use common experiences to instill in us the smallest seeds of doubt, delay, and distraction. We know this because of the evidence of his work in our own lives, but also in the lives of Paul and the early church.

Doubt

The early church: In his first letter to Timothy, Paul asked him to remind the wealthy Ephesian church to be content with what they had and to monitor what they were willing to do to get more (1 Tim. 6:17–19). Paul recognized that the pursuit of financial and material wealth could blind them to God's goodness, presence, and purpose, thus giving Satan a foothold.

Your life: You are scrolling through social media and notice an advertisement for Amazon. An influencer has posted her favorite household goods, and you realize that your own home now seems so uninspiring. You spend the next hour considering all the things you don't have—totally forgetting what you *do* have. In these moments, God's goodness is reduced to fragments. It may only look like online shopping, but what you are really doing is acting upon a misgiving, allowing Satan a foothold.

Reflection: In what instance have you compared yourself and your God-given resources to someone else and theirs? Did it cause you to doubt God's goodness toward you? What were you willing to do to acquire more for yourself?

Scripture: Scripture doesn't promise that the Lord will provide what we need in order to live comfortably, extravagantly, or just like our neighbor. We're told, instead, that the Lord will provide all that we need *in order to live for him* (Phil. 4:19).

Delay

The early church: Paul wrote two letters to the young Christians in Thessalonica, offering guidance and encouragement for their worldly struggles. Although his genuine concern for them was obvious, he couldn't visit a second time because Satan "prevented" it (1 Thess. 2:18 NLT). Paul didn't offer many details regarding Satan's work against him, but we can assume the unexpected "bumps in the road" were used to try and hinder Paul's missions. The good news? Paul did not allow Satan a foothold—he sent a letter instead! And not just any old letter—one so profound and encouraging to God's people that it's still being read some two thousand years later.

Your life: You are not currently attending church because, well, there are quite a few reasons. Your family has more important things to focus on right now, like travel ball. Your mom is sick and has frequented the intensive care unit. Church is thirty minutes from the house and feels totally out of the way. You will start going again when life slows down. But honestly, it probably never will, and all of a sudden, Satan has a foothold.

Reflection: When have minor inconveniences kept you from drawing near to God and being an asset to his kingdom? In the future, how can you patiently endure opposition, inconvenience, or Satan himself to ensure you are doing God's will?

Scripture: Truth, righteousness, peace, faith, salvation, "sword of the Spirit" (Eph. 6:17 NLT); put on God's armor to stand firm "against all strategies of the devil" (Eph. 6:11 NLT).

Distraction

The early church: In his letters to the church at Corinth, Paul urged them to keep Christ at the center of their lives so that the distractions they were facing did not give Satan a foothold (2 Cor. 11:3–4). The Corinthian church was known, among other things, for its inability to maintain a righteous way of life in a morally corrupt, ungodly culture.

Your life: Your husband recently got a promotion at work, and you're busy daydreaming about what that means for your house, your closet(s), your kids, your vacations. Before you know it, every penny was used to exceed your standard of living. You adjust well and wait for the next promotion, never considering what your God-given resources could've been used for outside of you—allowing Satan a foothold.

Reflection: Think of a time when you were too distracted by worldly pleasures or possessions to remember the Lord or the people he's placed in your proximity. How can you ensure it doesn't happen again?

Scripture: Concentrate not on the earthly, but the eternal—"the things of heaven" (Col. 3:2 NLT).

God has given us our abilities, influence, lifestyle, environment, and purpose so that we can use our opportunities to serve him and his people—for however long he's willing to use us. We didn't accumulate our material and financial wealth just to enjoy it. Our ability to create, teach, or encourage isn't random. We must acknowledge what he's given us and spend our lives giving it back.

My prayer is that God will make me brave enough to, next time, hang on for the long haul. There won't ever be a season of suffering, struggle, pain, or unbelief experienced this side of eternity that isn't worth our obedience and faithfulness to the Lord. Even if it looks like a silly basketball team. If I truly thought Jesus might arrive tomorrow, I would find a way to turn everything I had into praise. I would do everything for his glory. When we stand before God, I hope he doesn't have to ask us why, after hearing the gospel and giving our lives to him, we never made it a priority to follow through with a person who needed us, or more importantly, needed him. I sure don't want it to seem like we were inconvenienced by his plans or distracted by our own. I'm praying these things over you, sister friend, so that one day when you stand in his presence, he might call you a "good and faithful servant" (Matt. 25:23 NLT). This is the power of consistency.

— Questions —

1. Describe a time in your life when you experienced an inconvenience while trying to serve the Lord and his people. How did you react?

2. How can you start using each of the following to glorify God and serve his people?

   Ability:

   Influence:

   Lifestyle:

Environment:

Purpose:

3. Who in your life needs you to exemplify Jesus? How will you set aside doubts, delays, and distractions to make that person a priority?

Lord, I pray that we can reorganize our lives, starting with our everyday priorities, so that you can be the center focus. "Let us run with endurance the race God has set before us. We do this by keeping our eyes on Jesus, the champion who initiates and perfects our faith." (Heb. 12:1–2 NLT)

I pray, God, that you will provide a fresh sense of purpose and change our hearts to yearn for all that truly matters. "But my life is worth nothing to me unless I use it for finishing the work assigned me by the Lord Jesus—the work of telling others the Good News about the wonderful grace of God." (Acts 20:24 NLT)

I pray that we would be encouraged knowing that you, God, have already walked this road and are forever faithful. "Let us hold tightly without wavering to the hope we affirm, for God can be trusted to keep His promise." (Heb. 10:23 NLT)

Lord, may we offer every part of our lives to you— even the parts we think you don't care about. "Do not let sin control the way you live; do not give in to sinful desires. Do not let any part of your body become an instrument of evil to serve sin. Instead, give yourselves completely to God, for you were dead, but now you have new life." (Rom. 6:12–13 NLT)

NOTE

[1]Merriam-Webster *Dictionary Online*, s.v. "walk (*v.*)," accessed June 11, 2024, https://www.merriam-webster.com/dictionary/walk.

FOUR

A Letter on Love

A few years ago, Carson and I started talking about God's plan for our lives. We were enjoying married life and our apartment downtown, but neither of us really knew where it was going. We hadn't yet given much thought to starting a family but knew that, sooner or later, we'd have to decide. While we weren't sure whether we wanted to adopt a child or have our own, we opted to wait several years. Well, less than a month later, we found out that I was six weeks pregnant. This probably isn't the first (or last) time God has chuckled at my prayers.

They say that a baby changes everything, and maybe they really do. For me, though, the transition into motherhood felt more like a weird version of our old lifestyle and a strange new mixture of sleep deprivation, exhaustion, and diapers. It was almost unfair how much things changed but how much they also stayed the same. I walked into the hospital the last day of February feeling somewhat like my normal self and left twenty-four hours later with an eight-pound baby and a heart that had burst wide open. Arguably, for the first time in my life, I was experiencing a love completely untouched by or unrelated to the damaged world we live in. Even months later, the feeling continued to overflow inside of me, spilling out on other people, even strangers. I had become kinder and more patient. Stressed and spread thin, but happier. Slower to anger. Quicker to encourage.

I'll never fully understand the immediate, long-lasting change that took place in my soul. I hadn't realized, before, how closed off I had become in the years leading up to Riley's arrival—how impatient, unkind, self-protecting I had been toward others. I guess the world had crushed my spirit and, defensively, I had barricaded my heart. Maybe, on an instinctive level, I finally realized that being intolerant and closed off wasn't the kind of parent, friend, sister, or follower of Christ I wanted to be. Maybe having my own precious child, a son, put everything into perspective. I was able to see in a new way the depth of God's love for us. A love so perfect, selfless, and inconceivable it authored Jesus's death on the cross.

In my opinion, the salvation story has become fairly blasé. Even within the walls of the church, it's mentioned so casually. "Jesus died for our sins." "God sent his son." But do we allow ourselves to feel the gravity of it? Where did he send his son? To college? To Calvary? He sent his son *to the cross*, in our place, to suffer what is often referred to as the most excruciating type of death. The details, largely excluded from biblical accounts, are of no real interest to us. They're just too horrific, right? Yet, it's the details that make us feel the weight.

While at first I felt physically ill reading the specifics, I had to eventually stop studying so I could get out of my chair and onto my knees. I just wanted to lie on my face before Jesus and never get up again. I had either forgotten or never previously understood the extent to which he suffered or that he did so in careful obedience, for us. Jesus had power beyond our comprehension, but in that moment, he was human—and he suffered as such. While praying in the Garden of Gethsemane, Jesus's mind and body were under so much stress that he began to sweat blood (Luke 22:44). He knew what he was about to endure. This amount of fear would most likely cause the body to shut down or, at the very least, pass out. Jesus could've changed his mind or escaped the situation, but he didn't run. He allowed the religious leaders to arrest him, acknowledging that it was time "when the power of darkness reigns" (Luke 22:53 NLT).

Even before he was given the cross to carry, he was whipped, beaten, and spit on. A crown of thorns was placed on his head. The hair of his beard was pulled out. Eventually reaching Golgotha, he was stripped naked and laid atop the post. His wrists were fastened appropriately. This would've been done with nails about seven inches long.[1] When hoisted vertically to hang, his shoulders and elbows dislocated, causing his arms to "stretch to a minimum of six inches longer than their original length."[2] He began to suffocate. Some researchers believe that, due to his physical position on the cross as well as sustained trauma to his body, Jesus's lungs filled with fluid and his heart ruptured. This would make sense on account of the fact that, according to John 19:34 (NLT), "blood and water" poured from his side when it was pierced by the Roman soldier.

But, beyond this horror, Jesus was also experiencing spiritual death. "My God, my God, why have you forsaken me" (Matt. 27:46 NIV)? His last words on the cross suggest that while his body was physically separating from his soul, his spirit was also separating from that of the Father's. In the face of these gruesome details, I can't help but be ashamed. John R. W. Stott once said, "Before we can begin to see the cross as something done for us, we have to see it as something done by us."[3] We might not be the ones who betrayed Jesus, deserted him in that moment, or rolled dice for his clothing, but we are the ones who continue to live in sin, and that's ultimately what held him there.

Still, he said, "Father, forgive them, for they don't know what they are doing" (Luke 23:34 NLT). He died for us willingly; he had always known he would. On his last night with his disciples, Jesus broke bread and poured wine—a symbol of his body given, his blood poured out. A long-established sacrifice "to forgive the sins of many" (Matt. 26:28 NLT). Hours later, God fulfilled the promise—not only for them, but for us. In doing so, he gave us a chance to know him, love him, and spend eternity with him. Oh, to be Simon of Cyrene, the man forced to carry the cross when Jesus became too weak (Mark 15:21). I think carrying the cross of Jesus would become my life's greatest prize, knowing it was really only mine to carry in the first place.

I was rocking Riley to sleep one night—trying to memorize his heartbeat and the precious lines in his face—when suddenly, everything became clear, and the gravity of what Jesus had done, what his Father had ordained, settled into my soul. It occurred to me that while the Lord had taught me to love others better through my first experience as a mama, I would never, I mean never, trade Riley's life to save humanity. I still didn't love others *that* much. I've always known the world to be broken, but it often feels like there isn't any good left. No one is kind, nowhere is safe. People are rude, in a hurry, hurtful, dangerous. I simply wouldn't let my own son suffer and die so that undeserving people, me included, could be saved. How was God able to do it? Why did he want to?

Originally, I assumed this question was too overwhelmingly complex, not meant to be asked or understood. But really, the answer is simple. God stepped in while we were still sinners because he loves us and because he is love. Paul illustrated this in his letter to the Romans when he spoke about the reality of God. "He did not spare even his own son but gave him up for us" (Rom. 8:32 NLT). His love is sacrificial. In his letter to the church in Ephesus, Paul went on to say, "How wide and long and high and deep is the love of Christ" (Eph. 3:18 NIV). His love is unconditional, unending, unfathomable.

We aren't capable of loving this way, are we? I initially expected the answer to be no, primarily because we've come to know and understand the concept of love through an earthly lens, not a heavenly one. The kind of love we experience here doesn't always protect, trust, hope, or persevere. It isn't continuously selfless, slow to anger, patient, good-willed, or kind. Sometimes, love does fail. I was inclined to think we aren't capable of unconditional, unending, unfathomable, sacrificial love because we place a much greater weight in our identity as Americans, as wives, as mothers than we do in our identity as children of God. But, as it turns out, we *are* capable of loving people like Jesus does, most generally because we're made in his image (Gen. 1:27)—not just physically, but morally, spiritually, and intellectually. God set us apart from the rest of creation so we could willingly participate in the plans he has for us and for others. This means we have the capacity to feel joy, know peace, practice patience, spread kindness, reflect goodness, develop self-control, exemplify faithfulness, show gentleness, and yes, love others (Gal. 5:22–23) in an unconditional, unending, unfathomable, sacrificial way.

Here's something arguably more important: if we really are made in God's image, then that means every single person you encountered today was made by God, for God, and is worth so much to God that the Bible often compares them to our creator in both image and likeness. Okay! The secret is out. Not only can you now officially love people the right way, but there are officially people worth loving! Ha! The girl behind the counter who got your order wrong? Cherished by God, made in his image. The man driving the minivan that pulled out in front of you? Treasured by God, made in his likeness. The mutual friend you can't stand to be around? Your hurtful ex-boyfriend? Your toxic former boss? Your _____? Made in God's image, set apart for his purpose. These are the people we're called to love, even if they haven't chosen God or even chosen us.

Does it suddenly seem like God is asking too much? While he doesn't require us to give up a child—he made the final sacrifice by choosing to send his own—he does ask us to love our enemies, to pray for those who mistreat us, to lay down our lives for our friends, to "love each other as I have loved you" (John 15:12 NIV). And loving others like this isn't always effortless, especially when they've hurt us, disappointed us, or are simply strangers to us. What's more, society has organized us by race, religion, education, income, political party, ability, etc., and we let that drive who we feel we're capable of loving. Too many of us walk around with just enough patience to love people until it becomes inconvenient, uncomfortable, or seemingly too untidy for us.

What if God loved us this way? What if he loved us enough to help us get back on our feet but not enough to sit with us in our hurt? What if he loved us enough to stand beside us on the mountaintop but not enough to carry us through the valley? What if he loved us enough to want to rescue us but not enough to send his son in our place? There's so much to learn from this. Regardless of our inadequacies, our mishaps, and our offenses, he makes obvious his love for us by continuing to shepherd and sustain us (John 10:11). Surely we can't accept a love like this but not freely extend it to others. Wouldn't it be miserable trying to explain this to Jesus when we meet him?

God created us in his image so that while we go about our own lives, we'll also be able to put our careers, our goals—whatever secular purpose drives us—aside to propel ourselves in a direction of loving people better. Not just better, but unfathomably. With a type of love that isn't commanded by similarity, conventionality, or conditionality. With a type of love that threatens to crowd heaven. When Jesus says, "There is no greater love than to lay down one's life for one's friends" (John 15:13 NLT), he is referring to his act of love on the cross. But in the same sentence, he is also calling us to go just as far, to give up all that we have for others. Paul, in his letter to the Corinthian church, explained how he didn't make decisions based on what was best for him but on "what [was] best for others so that many may be saved" (1 Cor. 10:33 NLT). If you allow yourself to feel the joy and sincerity in these verses, if you let them reverberate through the inner workings of your spirit, you'll want to jump up, go out, and love someone else so largely it fails to make sense to either of you. Loving people is the mission.

To love *unconditionally* is to love without limits. If God sees the ugliness of our sin and chooses to love us through it, we can extend this type of love to others whether they change or stay the same. Proverbs 10:12 (NLT) says that "love makes up for all offenses."

To love *unendingly* is to love consistently, forever. God only deals with us from a place of love, and this is the lens through which we should view others. We are considered to be image bearers, and with this comes the responsibility to "do everything with love" (1 Cor. 16:14 NLT).

To love *unfathomably* is to love when it doesn't make sense. God loved us when we were still considered his enemy (Col. 1:21; Rom. 5:9–10), so we too can love others even when they've hurt or disappointed us. In fact, we're commanded to do so. "Love your enemies! Do good to those who hate you. Bless those who curse you. Pray for those who hurt you" (Luke 6:27–28 NLT).

To love *sacrificially* is to love without self-regard. Not even once did Jesus consider himself before he considered someone else. We're called to love our family this way too, and our friends, but also strangers and our enemies. Ephesians 5:21 (NLT) says, "Submit to one another out of reverence for Christ."

To not only give but to experience this type of love, we must first realize it won't be possible for us to do on our own. We must re-situate ourselves, adjust our posture. We need to release, willingly, our grip on the American dream. We must stop serving ourselves and focus on how we can serve—in Jesus's name—the people in our vicinity. Even if we have to skip dinner so our neighbor can eat. Even if we have to forgo a manicure so a stranger can fill their gas tank. Even if we miss our flight so a friend can have someone to sit with in their grief. An inconvenience in our eyes, a victory for heaven.

This is just a tiny glimpse of what it looks like to love people in the name of Jesus. I originally thought that I had been loving people this way all along, but as it turns out, I was wrong. How many disciples had I made with love that was self-serving? With love that was only given when it made sense? With love that was irregular, contingent? Instead, I'd most likely turned potential disciples *away* from the Christian faith by my poor example and hypocrisy. I'm thankful that God is sovereign and that, while he graciously allows us to participate in his work, we can't get in the way of all that he's doing.

— Questions —

1. Jot down an instance when you felt like you were able to love someone the way Jesus loves you.

2. Jot down an instance when you felt like you withheld love or acceptance because it wasn't comfortable or didn't make sense. What did God teach you in that moment?

Prayer

Father God, allow me to sit here for a moment and acknowledge my shortcomings and sin. Help me realize that I'm not deserving of your love or attention, but still, you pour it out on me in sacrificial, unfathomable ways. Thank you for loving me when it doesn't make sense. Please change the way I operate, shift my perspective, so that I can learn to love others well and, in turn, truly make disciples. I want to be used by you, God, and I know that the basis of kingdom work is loving people like you did.

NOTES

[1] David Terasaka, "Medical Aspects of the Crucifixion of Jesus Christ," Blue Letter Bible, https://www.blueletterbible.org/Comm/terasaka_david/misc/crucify.cfm.

[2] Cahleen Shrier, "The Science of the Crucifixion," Azusa Pacific University, March 1, 2002, https://www.apu.edu/articles/the-science-of-the-crucifixion/.

[3] John R. W. Stott, *The Cross of Christ* (Downers Grove, IL: InterVarsity Press, 2006), 53.

FIVE

Does God Trust You?

For a nation supposedly founded on Christian values, our ideologies surrounding success have nothing to do with loving others or loving the Lord. Categorically, even the American dream, no matter how you spin it, is both self- and object-oriented. We think, because of our distorted view of the gospel, that a lifestyle of this nature is acceptable—that we can have the American dream and Jesus too.

The American dream puts in front of us a finite choice of dreams and ambitions that are misaligned, misguided, and totally unrelated to the teachings of Jesus. We're made to believe that what's most "life-giving" has more to do with our chosen career path, income level, and social standing than it does with the one who gave life to us. We're taught to pursue happiness, not holiness. Tradition, not trustworthiness. While we may call ourselves followers of Christ, we often fail to live like followers should.

Why is it so hard for someone like me to trust God with her life? Is it because, in the United States, we're comfortable and don't really need to? Or because we think we'd make better decisions for ourselves and our families? Regardless of the reason(s), we've postured ourselves toward our creator in such a way that not only discounts his proximity but questions his trustworthiness. Do you think he questions ours? Or can he trust us with what he provides? I know I haven't been very trustworthy with the resources—the time, talent, people, purpose, and message—he's given me. So, maybe it isn't about trying to figure out if God is worthy of our trust but how we can be worthy of his.

We Pray and Seek God, but for the Wrong Things and Reasons

"You ask and don't receive because you ask with wrong motives, so that you may spend it on your pleasures" (James 4:3 CSB). The last time you prayed for a specific outcome, did you ask for his "will to be done" (Matt. 26:39 NLT)? Did you ask him to prepare you for his plans instead of your own? We are encouraged to bring our requests to God—even when our prayers are doused in emotion or we're not thinking clearly. God wants to hear each one because he loves us, but if your prayers reflect your narrow mind and crooked heart they, in all likelihood, won't get answered. The Lord doesn't look upon our selfish desires and smile.

We Work Not for the Kingdom, but for Ourselves

Just like our nonbelieving neighbors, we spend most of our lives working, not only to survive here, but because we want to thrive here, too. While God wants us to work and do so joyfully, he never intended for it to become an unhealthy obsession or vain compulsion. Nor does he want the results of our work to be wholly self-serving. The way in which we overwork ourselves suggests we think we're on our own, even though it's illustrated in Philippians 4:19 that he "will supply all [our] needs from his glorious riches" (NLT). Do we assume that this isn't true or that it doesn't apply to us? Or do we simply reject the idea because what he's given doesn't seem good enough?

We Pursue Excess

We're told again, in 2 Corinthians 9:8 (NLT), that we will "always have everything [we] need"—even some left over to share with others. What exactly was Paul referring to when he said, "everything we need"? Where does enough end and surplus begin? The American dream tells us we need a beach house, a luxury car, an incredible career. The prosperity "gospel" essentially tells us the same—that Jesus even wants this for us, but that isn't true. Although sometimes God gives in excess, we were never meant to *live* in excess. With every promotion and pay bump, Carson and I always found a new way to spend money. We would buy the nicer version of something; we'd officially "upgrade." "Everything we needed" became convoluted in the blessing. We were working to "have it all," not to share it all. John Piper says it best: "It's not a sin to make a lot of money, it's a sin to want to keep a lot of money."[1]

We Let Temptation Control Us

Materialistic is defined as being "excessively concerned with physical comforts or the acquisition of wealth and material possessions, *rather than with* spiritual, intellectual, or cultural values."[2] The definition itself implies you can't have the American dream and Jesus too. See how serious this is? James 5:3 (NLT) even says that the "treasure you have hoarded will testify against you on the day of judgment." If you've chosen to store your treasures here on Earth, you're most likely considered untrustworthy in the eyes of the Lord.

If you aren't sure you've been trustworthy, you need to look at two things: your willing obedience and your wealth. There's a whole chapter about obedience in this book because it's just so crucial. For now, however, let me just say this: if you've been drifting along, completely unaware of what God's doing in your life, then there's no way you've been obedient. A forgotten God isn't a followed one. And if you're not being obedient, you're not being trustworthy.

Second, your wealth. It took me feeling like we were in a good place financially to realize that the wealthier we became, the less we depended on Jesus and the less time we spent in his presence. We had money to spend not only on "stuff" but on experiences (stockpiling his blessings will keep you busier than you think). Why weren't we keeping enough for our family and giving the rest back to heaven? Were we only giving 10 percent because, suddenly, 10 percent seemed like a lot? After these questions came up, I felt trapped. Our lifestyle would have to change. We'd have to downsize, trade in, get rid of. Was I willing to do this in order to re-situate my life? To fix my posture and turn my gaze toward heaven?

If you're a "normal" person, if you've established a life that looks like everyone else's, you're most likely bothered by this book. I was bothered just writing it because I like material possessions and have been taught to acquire them. To give up anything that provides a sense of protection or pleasure goes against everything my flesh desires. But as a follower of Christ, I also know I'm not supposed to live the way that I do—even in one of the most affluent countries in the world.

You may be willing to sell your boat and write a check to your favorite organization. You might be willing to trade in your fancy car for a minivan and free up some cash to help your neighbor. But what if you aren't willing to downsize your house or uproot your family or change jobs? In 2 Kings 15:34, Jotham did what was right in the Lord's sight, except destroy the pagan idols. Not only was this partial obedience, but pagan idols also translate, in today's time, to wealth, comfort, and security.

Don't lounge about, assuming you're right with God. If you've made something—even unknowingly—off-limits to him, you've marked yourself as unreliable, and he'll choose not to trust you. We can't blame him for this. We wouldn't trust him either if he withheld his best from us. The extensive resources he provides, the infinite blessings he pours out from heaven, belonged to him first. Frankly, they still belong to him. They won't, at any point, belong to *us*. If God supplied you with extra money so you could turn it into a blessing for someone else and, instead, you bought a second home or Botox or Louis Vuitton, you proved yourself to be untrustworthy. You chose happiness over holiness, Earth over eternity. If you're coveting a friend's lifestyle; if you're obsessing over your new car; or if you're arrogant, greedy, or ambitious for the wrong reasons, you are neglecting the work and will of God. You're misusing the time, talent, money, and people in your life. Do you think God will trust you enough to give you more?

Here's where things get weird: if you haven't already, you'll most likely soon stumble across Christians who live this way. These Christians are everywhere; they are all of us. Maybe they're active in church. Maybe they post Bible verses online each morning. Yet, they also act like their resources solely belong to them. What's confusing is this: we witness these same people continue to acquire more. We accept, because they're our fellow brothers and sisters in Christ, that this is God's continued blessing, and most likely, they do too. But doesn't it actually seem more like a coincidence, a result of earthly striving? Isn't it possible that we're all somehow, in our own way, slightly complacent, disobedient, and untrustworthy? We must question if Satan uses our situations to keep us unaware of our unfaithfulness.

So, is it even possible, because of our sinful nature, for the Lord to trust us? Why would he want to? In spite of our feelings, the Bible does, in fact, use the word *entrust* to clarify God's expectations. He is trusting us to care for the Earth and everything in it (Gen. 1:28). He is counting on us to carry the good news of the gospel to the ends of the Earth (2 Tim. 1:14). Yet the question remains: Are we being trustworthy? As American Christians, do we even know how to be?

How to Be Trustworthy

Below are several practical ways that we can be trustworthy in our lives. Some people will assume that to truly be trustworthy, they'll have to sell everything they own and move to the Middle East tomorrow. Other people will excuse away this assumption because they aren't willing to do so. God has a unique purpose for each of us, but we can't assume that our purpose fits neatly inside the confines of the American dream. If we genuinely consider ourselves followers of Christ, shouldn't we be carrying the gospel to the ends of the earth, caring for widows, orphans, and the poor until God tells us otherwise? The Bible makes clear the work and will of God, yet a lot of us, feeling like we haven't yet heard from him directly, choose to pursue our own interests—and if we aren't able to be trusted with little, he'll never trust us with much (Luke 16:10).

If you're starting to feel overwhelmed, I pray you also feel the countless prayers of peace I've prayed over your life. The Lord doesn't want you to be burdened by his work—he doesn't require it for the salvation of your soul. However, the fact that your soul was saved by God should propel you into an unending season of joy, of fruitfulness, of trustworthiness. Let's start where we are with what we have. Let's do what we can today to leverage ourselves for the kingdom of God. Time, money, sphere of influence, purpose, lifestyle—these things look different for each of us. But if we fully surrender our hearts to God and with it everything else, he will help us make the necessary changes to become trustworthy with the small things. And hopefully, one day, we'll be trustworthy enough for the big ones.

With Your Time

The concept of time is tough for us. We put deadlines and time restraints on our requests to God, and because his timing often doesn't overlap with our own, we then wrestle with feelings of frustration, uncertainty, and abandonment. Yet, how can we ask the God of the universe to turn in his work by Friday at five? If we want to be trustworthy, we have no choice but to stop worrying about his timing and what it means for us. Rather, we should focus on the time we do understand and how we can use it wisely for his purposes. According to Billy Graham, we can do this in four ways.[3]

To start, we can choose to see each day for what it is—a gift. "Time isn't exhaustible, nor can we assume we'll always have more; someday our time on Earth will end." If we truly realized this, our priorities would inevitably rearrange themselves, and we would never be too busy or too bored for God. Second, we can commit our time to God. Graham says, "God gave it to you for a reason; not to be wasted or mishandled, but to be used for His glory. We are accountable to Him for the way we use our time, and once a minute passes it can never be reclaimed." Third, we can set aside time for God. Not our spare time, but our first and freshest moments. Last, Graham states that it's okay to take time for our own needs. "[Jesus] said to [his] disciples, 'Come with me by yourselves to a quiet place and get some rest'" (Mark 6:31 NIV).

Additionally, we would benefit from observing the Sabbath. While there is much debate on the topic, most people generally agree that the purpose of the Sabbath is to be still, to rest, to "practice for eternity in God's presence."[4] It might not be sinful to spend your Sunday afternoon watching football, catching up on work, grocery shopping, or meal prepping. But, if you aren't making an even greater effort to seek and spend time with God, to be in his presence, then you're not being faithful.

With Your Money

"A man [was] going on a long trip. He called together his servants and entrusted his money to them while he was gone. He gave five bags of silver to one, two bags of silver to another, and one bag of silver to the last—dividing it in proportion to their abilities. He then left on his trip" (Matt. 25:14–15 NLT). If you were to read the story in its entirety, you would see that while the man was away, the servants did with the money what they thought was best. Two of them chose to invest it, and ultimately, both of them ended up with more. One servant took the money and buried it. He didn't lose any of it, but he didn't multiply it either. The moral of the story? The way we're using our resources, or the way we're choosing not to use them, is a direct reflection of our trustworthiness, our readiness for the Lord's return.

Although in the Bible we see God take pleasure in wealthy people—such as King Solomon, Queen Esther, King David—we're also plainly told that it's hard for rich people to get into heaven (Matt. 19:24). In fact, the possession of riches is sometimes even considered a spiritual liability. Why? Because usually, it's not a lack of money that keeps us from giving; it's an overabundance of money that does so. There truly is danger in plenty. Excess makes us forget how much we need God but also how much we desire him. When we're wealthy enough to fix our problems, when we're privileged enough to not only buy whatever we need but whatever we want, when we're fortunate enough to feel secure and happy, we forget who God is. And when we forget God, it's impossible for us to be obedient and trustworthy. Something else takes his place, and we swiftly circle back to idolatry.

We can't forget that if we find ourselves in a place of abundance, it's because God entrusted us to be there (Deut. 8:18). Even though he blesses us, we're told to "honor the LORD" with our wealth and with "the best part of everything" we produce (Prov. 3:9 NLT). One of the earliest Bible stories illustrates this well. When it was time for the harvest, Cain and Abel offered gifts to the Lord. Cain presented some of his crops, while Abel brought the finest of his flock (Gen. 4:3–7). The Lord accepted Abel's gift, but we're told he had no respect for Cain. In my own experience, it appears we're more like Cain than we are like Abel. We may offer gifts to God, but typically only when we have enough to spare.

Rick Warren, author of *The Purpose Driven Life*, said in a 2015 interview that he and his wife "reverse tithe."[5] Instead of giving 10 percent to God, they give 90 percent. He said, "Every time I give, it breaks the grip of materialism in my life. Every time I give, it makes me more like Jesus." Although he's a prominent author and church leader, he says that he's lived in the same house for fifteen years, he still drives the same Ford truck, and he wears the same two suits. Francis Chan, in a sermon titled "The Truth About Tithing," has also broached the topic. Ultimately, he doesn't believe that we're commanded to give a certain amount of our income. As followers of Christ, we should have the same desire as Christ, and that is to give and to do so cheerfully. We shouldn't share our resources out of guilt or obligation but because "we're inheritors of God's glorious riches and we want to treat others the way he so graciously treats us."[6]

I look at these two men and think, "Wow, they're right!" No matter the size of your income, 10 percent is only a tiny portion of what you've been given. After mulling this over, Carson and I revisited our finances. We were offering 10 percent of our income to the Lord. We knew that and were proud of it, but when we realized we were spending more on our monthly mortgage, when we concluded that a higher percentage was going to our retirement, there was no longer a way for us to pretend we were participating in the real work of Jesus. We were giving back to God, sure, but largely, we were storing up treasure in the wrong place.

Second Corinthians 9:6 (ESV) says, "Whoever sows sparingly will also reap sparingly, and whoever sows bountifully will also reap bountifully." This makes sense to us, right? I mean, duh. If we don't study for an exam, we aren't going to ace it. If we don't invest money in the market, we won't get a return. If we don't store up treasure in heaven, there will be nothing there for us when we die. How can we feel compelled to give only 10 percent after everything he's done for us?

With Your Sphere of Influence

If you're anything like the rest of us, there are people in your life right now—coworkers, family members, mutual friends—who you wish would just go away. People you may find to be annoying, hurtful, awkward, weird. In fact, as much as I hate to admit it, every time we meet a new person, we decide (even subconsciously) whether we want to pursue a relationship or interact with them again. This, of course, starts at a young age. We're taught to be very selective in relationships—not just with our friends, but any of the people we welcome into our lives. This is, to an extent, healthy. However, it's also important to remember that every single person we meet can benefit from the love of Jesus demonstrated through us. You don't have to be best friends with these people, or really even like them, but you do have to love them—because that's not complicated, is it?! And whether we like it or not, we don't get to choose who God calls us to. Jesus, in giving the Great Commission, didn't specify a certain type of identity or nationality.

He didn't say to love *only* your closest friends or your mother. He used the term "all nations"—and that means all nationalities and races. Both political parties. Each social class. Every personality type. Your enemies! (Matt. 28:16–20).

Not only have we closed ourselves off to certain types of people, but we also don't love the people in our inner circle well either. We use prayer requests as an excuse to gossip about their lives and problems. We love "unconditionally" until they make a bad decision or simply a decision that goes against our own beliefs and wishes. We criticize them. We complain about their faults and flaws—and we do all of this in light of how Jesus chose to love *us*. We're too busy working to acquire friends who love us, colleagues who respect us, kids who befriend us, to truly take inventory of the people in our lives. What kind of person do they need you to be? A self-centered, critical, materialistic one? Or one whom Jesus deems trustworthy?

With Your Purpose

I spent my first year of graduate school in a higher education program at a prominent school in Tennessee. I learned, fairly quickly, that our society was pivoting in such a way that rendered a Christian, heterosexual woman offensive and unethical. I was told by my peers that the very thing I embodied had become "outdated," "irrelevant," and "privileged into oblivion," and I "had nothing to bring to the table." Although I wanted to run, I also felt challenged to be a light, to be the salt God had intended me to be. Instead, I really did put "a basket over my lamp" (Matt. 5:15) for the sake of being professional and politically correct. I wasn't trustworthy with the message God had given me.

God has given all of us a story. Not only the truth and the hope of the story he authored, but how it profoundly impacts our lives and saves our souls. It's a message worth sharing at every low point, every rock bottom, but also at every high spot, every pinnacle. We should be singing in the streets, witnessing in the classrooms, and preaching in the prisons, but we keep it to ourselves. We're too afraid of seeming unethical or offensive. In the midst of this, we must remind ourselves that God didn't give us a purpose so we could keep silent. Time is running out, day by day, for all of us. Shouldn't we urgently be telling people about their Savior? Shouldn't it feel like our calling, the point of our existence? Sure, the political and cultural climate of our nation has made this harder to do, but it's not impossible. The disciples and the early church had a much more uncomfortable, threatening time doing so—and did it just the same.

With Your Lifestyle

We all experience seasons of intentional serving—motherhood, ministry, missions. Yet some people seem to have a "life" purpose that spans longer than just a certain period of time. It's clear, to them and to us, that it's more than just a phase. No matter what our specific purpose looks like, the point of our lives is to know the Lord and serve him well. But time and again, we aren't trustworthy with our purpose because we're too worried about what everyone else is doing with theirs.

You might be a well-known author and speaker, your sphere of influence obvious and exciting. You might be a high school English teacher, your sphere of influence smaller, but just as evident and just as powerful. Or maybe you're a stay-at-home mom, and your sphere of influence is just two or three little people. In your eyes, your job isn't as thrilling or impactful as that of your friends, the teacher, and the author. I get it, and so does God. But, at the end of the day, this isn't an appropriate way to measure your worth, or even the worth of your friends. Nor is it fair to you, your friends, or God to completely disregard the biblical concept of "his hands and feet" (Matt. 22:13 NLT). God uses all of us together to complete his will and his work, and the way God chooses to use us is for him to decide; the fruit of our labor is for him to determine. We must only be obedient with what he has given.

When we had Riley, our lifestyle changed. Not only because I quit my job and our income was cut in half, but because we welcomed a new, precious life that depended on us for everything. A pattern of life can change for a number of different reasons: income, health, family, career. Regardless of your lifestyle or if it's recently changed, all of ours differ, and it's our job to decide how we're going to use every aspect of it to glorify God and be an asset to his kingdom. What consumes you? What do you spend your time on? Where do you live? Do you have a job? If so, how do you get to work? Are you a shopaholic or a minimalist? Are you living within your means or continuously overspending? Did you inherit wealth or acquire your own? What do you wear? What do you eat? We all have a carefully curated lifestyle that remains largely unaffected by Christ until we offer it to him and ask to be made worthy of his trust.

Trustworthy in the eyes of the Lord is something we have to become. We can't snap our fingers and suddenly just *be*. If our hearts truly seek trustworthiness, if we genuinely strive to be loyal and forever connected to God, he'll make us so. First Corinthians 10:31 (CSB) says, "Do everything for the glory of God." We don't get to define for ourselves what "everything" means. It means that with any and all things, we glorify him. And that's made possible when we become good stewards of what he's given. Not only giving him credit for the blessing, but by using the blessing wisely.

Trustworthy in the Eyes of the Lord

Abraham was trustworthy. We're told in Genesis 22 that Abraham was willing to sacrifice Isaac, his son, as an offering—just because God asked. He couldn't have possibly understood God's reasoning but chose to be carefully obedient. Abraham was confirming his trustworthiness. As a result, God promised to greatly multiply and bless his descendants.

Job was trustworthy. "Then the LORD asked Satan, 'Have you noticed my servant Job? He is the finest man in all the earth. He is blameless—a man of complete integrity. He fears God and stays away from evil.' Satan replied to the LORD, 'Yes, but Job has good reason to fear God. You have always put a wall of protection around him and his home and his property. You have made him prosper in everything he does. Look how rich he is! But reach out and take away everything he has, and he will surely curse you to your face!'" (Job 1:8–10 NLT). Soon after, Job experienced devastating loss. His livestock, his servants, his children—everything was taken in a matter of what seemed like minutes. But Job didn't react like Satan thought he would. While of course Job grieved, he also "fell to the ground to worship" the Lord (Job 1:20 NLT). Job actually endured months of testing, and while he questioned God, he never cursed him. God was sure of Job's faith, and Job confirmed he was able to be trusted.

Jesus was trustworthy. We know that God is three in one—he's the Holy Spirit, he's the Father, and he's the Son. Yet, we're told in Philippians 2:6 (NLT) that when Jesus walked the Earth, he did not "cling to" his equality with God but gave up his divine privileges by being born human. Jesus trusted the Father (Heb. 2:13), even while on the cross. If this is possible, can't we also assume that God considered Jesus to be trustworthy? Ultimately, Jesus was sent by God to complete the greatest mission of all, and he did so as a human with free will.

The apostle Paul was trustworthy. He said so himself. "I thank Christ Jesus our Lord, who has given me strength to do his work. He considered me trustworthy and appointed me to serve him" (1 Tim. 1:12 NLT). Wouldn't you like to be able to say this, too? Paul went from persecuting Christians to being killed for his faith. He turned from his sin and willfully sacrificed everything to follow God. He walked in obedience.

Prayer

Father God, I praise your name. I sit here in awe of how wonderful and trustworthy you are. You keep your promises, and you love us in unfathomable ways. Help me to remember your example as I try to become trustworthy in your eyes. I no longer want to live for myself or waste the resources you have given me. I want to be a good steward so that you may be glorified and pleased with my life.

NOTES

[1]John Piper, "Why I Abominate the Prosperity 'Gospel,'" Desiring God, YouTube video, 10:34, October 27, 2009, https://www.youtube.com/watch?v=jLRue4nwJaA.

[2]Dictionary.com, s.v. "materialistic" (*adj.*), accessed June 20, 2024, https://www.dictionary.com/browse/materialistic#—emphasis added.

[3]Billy Graham, "In His Own Words—Billy Graham: 4 Steps to Using Your Times More Wisely," *Blog from the Billy Graham Library*, January 17, 2014, https://billygrahamlibrary.org/in-his-own-words-billy-graham-4-steps-to-using-your-time-more-wisely/.

[4]Missy Takano, "What Is the Sabbath in the Bible and Should Christians Observe It?," BibleProject, January 6, 2020, https://bibleproject.com/articles/keeping-the-sabbath-is-it-still-relevant-to-christians-today/.

[5]"Rick Warren's Second Transformation," Beliefnet, https://www.beliefnet.com/faiths/christianity/2005/10/rick-warrens-second-reformation.aspx.

[6]Francis Chan, "The Truth about Tithing," YouTube video, 5:25, July 9, 2017, https://www.youtube.com/watch?v=4cs0gRxzKpY.

SIX

Junior League *Jesus*

"Casual Christianity" is defined in George Barna's book *The Seven Faith Tribes* as "the desire to please God, family, and other people while extracting as much enjoyment and comfort from the world as possible."[1] Barna, in the same passage, goes on to say that success to a casual Christian "means balancing everything 'just right' to maximize opportunities and joys in life without undermining perceived relationship with God and others." According to Barna's studies, 66 percent of the adult population in the United States are casual Christians—that's two out of three people.[2] An alarming statistic, but it's one I have, unfortunately, probably always identified with.

If the punishment required for our well-being really did fall on Jesus, and if by his wounds we really are healed (Isa. 53:5), how can any of us respond in a manner that suggests it's casual? Are we truly unable to comprehend the magnitude of what he did? Or has life in the waiting worn us down to the point of complacency?

While I'd like to ignore Barna's data because it's distressing, I also feel an overwhelming sense of responsibility to change it. I've spent my whole life surrounded by differing levels of Christianity, but I've yet to find someone who has surrendered every part of their life to Jesus, who has relinquished control without having a backup plan or safety net. Like any casual Christian, I want to know Jesus, but I also want to enjoy life and keep spending my time, energy, and money the way I always have. In the book of Matthew, Jesus talks to a rich man who has inquired about eternal life. He tells the man to "keep the commandments . . . sell all your possessions and give the money to the poor . . . then come, follow me" (Matt. 19:17–22 NLT). Ultimately, the man turned away sad, but he turned away nonetheless, "for he had many possessions." He chose what was earthly over what was eternal. We also don't seem interested in turning the American dream on its head. After all, what's the alternative? Losing our false sense of security?

We turn away, just like the rich man, and continue to stay busy, justifying our lifestyle choices by arguing that "the gospel is needed in my workplace, my social circle." While we might be right about this—God can use us anywhere if we're willing—we usually aren't doing anything about it. It just serves as an excuse for our comfort—an afterthought regarding the life we've already assembled—and it's watering down the gospel. It's misconstruing it to the point that it no longer holds us to a standard that's beyond ourselves and our tendencies. We simply are who we are: *it is what it is.* And we'll never be who God intended if we keep this up.

John Piper once said that there are millions of Christians who think they're heaven bound who really are not—people "for whom Christ is at the margins of their thoughts and affections, not the transforming center."[3] If God truly were at the center of your being, if he held the most powerful place in your heart, things would probably look different than they do in this moment. You might have a different job or live in a different city. Your closet might not be as full, and your house might not be as nice. You may have watered down the gospel or created your own version of it. As casual Christians, we do that.

We tend to only highlight the qualities of God that we benefit from—love, forgiveness, mercy—further legitimizing the idea that we are too loved, too treasured, too worthy of saving to be separated from him. And if you keep God on the outskirts of your heart, you'll convince yourself that a lifestyle of "insignificant" and "inconsistent" sin isn't that big of an issue because Jesus will love and choose you anyway. After all, we're told that nothing can separate us from God. We are his most prized possession! We are enough!

We water down the gospel by choosing our own truth. We maintain our commitment to sin and secularity by pretending we are safe. We underestimate our desperate need for Jesus by downplaying our helplessness. Jeremiah asked the crowd at the temple gates if they were going to steal, murder, commit adultery, swear falsely, burn incense to other gods, and then come "before Me in this house, which is called by My Name, and say 'We are protected *and* set free [by this act of religious ritual]!'—only to go on with this wickedness *and* these disgusting and loathsome things?" (Jer. 7:10 AMP—square brackets in the original). They were essentially doing whatever they wanted in hopes that their sin would be overlooked because of their observances in the temple. In similar fashion, we steal, hate, gossip, and worship idols, all the while considering ourselves to be safe because we prayed the sinner's prayer or were baptized as babies.

While the Lord really does love us, treasure us, and want to take us to heaven, we can't forget Jesus's words in Matthew 7:21 (NLT): "I never knew you. Depart from me, you lawbreakers!" Or Paul's words in Romans 3:23 (NLT): "For everyone has sinned; we all fall short of God's glorious standard." We can't afford to be complacent. It is in our dwelling and abiding *in* him that keeps us from eventually being separated *from* him. And when we draw near, the power of sin and the attractiveness of the American dream grow dim, rendering themselves worthless, and we're able to finally get to the root of what it means to live for Jesus.

Jia Tolentino, a writer for *The Guardian*, describes the ideal woman in her article "Athleisure, barre and kale":

> She's of indeterminate age but resolutely youthful presentation. She's got glossy hair and the clean, shameless expression of a person who believes she was made to be looked at. She is often luxuriating when you see her—on remote beaches, under stars in the desert, across a carefully styled table, surrounded by beautiful possessions or photogenic friends. The ideal woman steps into a stratum of expensive juices, boutique exercise classes, skincare routines and vacations, and there she happily remains.[4]

Nothing but looks and luxury. Was it wrong of me to assume that this woman, who by all standards is perfect, can't possibly be a follower of Christ? While I feel poor, fat, and friendless (and now judgmental) compared to this woman, we probably have more in common than I think. She very well could be a casual Christian, just like me. Statistically, she's more likely than not to identify as one. Although I can only financially afford to do so on a lesser scale, I find myself wanting to spend more time enjoying God's blessings than I do wanting to serve or acknowledge him.

Yet, someone who has even less than I do might look at me the way I look at this ideal woman. We're all striving to acquire more. More opportunities, more possessions, more experiences. We're all just having to start from a different place. Whether or not we choose to admit it, most of us care about vacations, luxury cars, skin care, and designer bags. We try to "keep up with the Kardashians,"[5] our neighbors, our kids' friends' parents. We covet invitations to exclusive organizations like sororities, country clubs, and the Junior League—ones whose membership requirements hardly reach beyond wealth, status, and beauty.

Some of these organizations claim to have Christian backgrounds, but that's often a feel-good, Southern thing. The individuals that make up these groups may host events and perform philanthropy, but they're also required to maintain the "image," the standard of what a member looks and acts like. A little weight gain, a loss of income, a public embarrassment, and you're no longer accepted. Karen Hendricks, the Junior League lobbyist on Capitol Hill, says the Junior League was once reserved for "the white, upper-middle-income woman who doesn't work outside the home, has two kids and a Volvo."[6] Seriously? A Volvo? You can't make this stuff up! While the Junior League has significantly evolved, the stereotype remains. Back in the late 1970s, *Texas Monthly* described it as "exclusively educational, charitable and to promote volunteerism," but the author also mentioned talks of "dieting, dyslexia, designer dresses, and divorce."[7]

The Junior League specifically may not be associated with Christianity or its values, but it serves as an example of a collection of women who are doing good work, women who are on the right track, but lose sight of themselves because of worldly expectations and what the American dream tells them their lives should look like. But you know what group *is* supposedly associated with Christianity and its values? A sort of pre–Junior League organization: the collegiate sorority. Although these groups claim to be rooted in Christianity, they host rituals, require oaths, and largely glorify themselves. Additionally, they're known for "upholding an elitist class system and creating an unfair advantage in universities" while undertaking charity work and reciting Scripture to "maintain the good girl image."[8]

If you've seen the hashtag Bama Rush on any of your social media platforms (or seen the documentary *Bama Rush*), you probably know that while these organizations tend to advertise themselves as followers of Christ, they choose not to accept people the way Jesus would have. Maybe the standards aren't written in stone, but it's obvious that, to receive a bid, you need to be gorgeous, thin, popular, and rich. If you're not all these things, you're at least three of them. In a post that recently went viral, a sorority hopeful showcased the outfit she would be wearing for the second day of rush festivities. Between Cartier, David Yurman, and Burberry, viewers soon realized her outfit cost roughly $25,000. This is the culture of many women in our country, and unfortunately, this vibe, these expectations, also bleed over into circles that claim to be crazy about Jesus.

The week before I was slated to speak for the first time at church, I went and got my nails done and bought a new outfit—a bright pink blazer, white wash jeans, and platform sneakers. I spent a bit more time on my makeup and hair that morning to ensure that I looked my best so I could feel my best. God had put a message on my heart, and I felt called to share it. But I also wanted to look good doing it. I wanted to appear put together and pretty; I wanted an attractive appearance so people would be interested in what I had to say. While getting dressed, my husband came into the bathroom and, after appraising my outfit, said, "You officially look like a Christian influencer." I made a face at him and laughed it off, but he was right. I did look the part. And in my opinion, there shouldn't be a "part" here to physically look like.

If you're connected on social media to any well-known Christian leaders who are women—writers, speakers, well-known pastor's wives—you've probably noticed the inner workings of their personal lives. Many of them get Botox, lip fillers, cellulite reduction, light therapy. They drive Range Rovers and live in gated communities. They share glimpses of their glamorous lifestyles, including their trips to Europe, their perfectly curated houses at Christmas, their name-brand clothes, and their frequent spa visits. Their lives look like the Instagram influencer on the next screen over, yet these are the people doing the work of Jesus.

I used to look at some of these women and think, "Gosh, I want to be just like her!" I wanted to be wealthy. I wanted to be pretty, to have a "pretty" life. But, at the end of the day, I still wasn't convinced it was okay to use the resources God had given me to buy myself a luxurious life. Women who are looking for a faithful friend, a godly example, notice this, and it leads them to believe that this type of lifestyle, this gross misuse of God's resources, is acceptable and celebrated by God.

Don't get me wrong: Jesus expects us to be responsible with the resources he gives, and while using them to serve others is Christlike, he also wants us to use them to meet the needs of ourselves and our families. However, I also think that we take self-care extremely out of context by continually justifying massages, manicures, mini-vacations—things that are above and beyond what we actually need. We're too busy worrying about our feelings to realize that true self-care happens when we sit before the Lord, when we ask him to refine our hearts, our thoughts, the areas of our lives we haven't yet surrendered. When we care for ourselves this way, our houses may not be as tidy, our bodies may not be as pretty, but our souls will be headed toward heaven, and that's the best self-care of all. That's the biblical essence of an ideal woman.

If the book of Proverbs uses godly character and reverence for the Lord as a means to measure beauty and value, why do we let our worth hinge on how our bodies look, how we present them? Why do we spend so much time trying to make ourselves worthy of the world and not enough time trying to make ourselves worthy of the life he's called us to (Eph. 4:1)? When I'm standing in the bathroom pouting and telling my husband, "I can't go, I don't know what to wear, I'm having a clothes crisis," this actually exposes the condition of my heart.

Have I forgotten that these things don't matter to heaven? We're told in 1 Peter 3:3–4 (NLT) not to be "concerned about the outward beauty of fancy hairstyles, expensive jewelry, or beautiful clothes." Instead, we should be worried about what really makes us beautiful: our character. If this directive isn't enough to convince us, we're also told in Isaiah that all the physical things that make us beautiful will eventually be stripped away.

> On that day of judgment, the Lord will strip away everything that makes her beautiful: ornaments, headbands, crescent necklaces, earrings, bracelets, and veils; scarves, ankle bracelets, sashes, perfumes, and charms; rings, jewels, party clothes, gowns, capes, and purses; mirrors, fine linen garments, head ornaments, and shawls. (Isa. 3:18–23 NLT)

Thank God he didn't mention shoes. Kidding! But only slightly.

All joking aside, shouldn't we lessen our grip on the stuff we've been told we *need*? The jumpsuits, the wedges, the "on-trend" loungewear. Shouldn't we be more concerned about clothing ourselves in the armor of God? I'm serious! When I finally get to meet him, the Gucci belt I just had to have will suddenly no longer matter. What will matter is this: "the belt of truth" (Eph. 6:10 NLT), the "body armor of God's righteousness" (Eph. 6:14 NLT), the "shield of faith" (Eph. 6:16 NLT), "salvation as your helmet" (Eph. 6:17 NLT), and the "sword of the Spirit" (Eph. 6:17 NLT), and what I was able to do for God's kingdom once I was fully dressed.

A decades-old article published in the *Los Angeles Times* talks about shopping addictions. The woman who was interviewed detailed her shopping problem by explaining that she had a secret stash of credit cards and a post office box that her husband didn't know about. "I make as much money as my husband . . . . If I want a $500 suit from Ann Taylor, I deserve it and don't want to be hassled about it. So, the easiest thing to do is lie."[9] To an extent, we do the same thing to God. We use our "own" resources (which are really his in the first place) to purchase things we think we deserve, and we try to hide it by making it look like the problem doesn't exist. Our society, of course, fuels the fire by normalizing this behavior.

Of course, the issue isn't only about how we present our bodies; it's about our bodies themselves. Contrary to popular belief, you can be flabby. Your nail polish can be chipped. Your skin can be wrinkly, scarred, tattooed, because it's not what's on the outside that defines you. God only cares about your heart. While your body is a temple and he wants you to treat it as such, he doesn't add or withhold acceptance based on outward appearance (1 Sam. 16:7). Does this take the pressure off? Honestly, it probably doesn't. Our culture has severely brainwashed us with its own definition and standard of beauty, and it has nothing to do with our hearts. If you've worn makeup for even one day, you know what I'm talking about. The slogan for L'Oréal? "Because you're worth it." Sephora? "The beauty authority." Estée Lauder? "Defining beauty." Chanel? "Where beauty begins." Although these slogans aren't entirely obtrusive, they lead us to believe, at least on a subliminal level, that beauty is physical, that makeup is what makes you attractive, that certain brands are what make you worthy. We haven't made space for a lesser standard, but we need to because Jesus did. After all, we're the only ones who think that physical standards matter.

When Jesus walked the Earth, he rubbed shoulders with people who were sick, paralyzed, deformed. He knew that, because of sin, creation would forever suffer. The human body was no longer perfect as he created it to be. It ages, most of the time ungracefully. It contracts disease. It becomes disabled, misshapen. This owes to the fact that sin itself is a disease, a disability, an awfully ugly thing. Isn't it time we accept this for what it is and stop killing ourselves in the pursuit of physical perfection? We're told that when Jesus returns, we'll be given new, glorious bodies. First Corinthians 15:43 (NLT) says, "Our bodies are buried in brokenness, but they will be raised in glory. They are buried in weakness, but they will be raised in strength." See? Has anyone ever told you that your body is glorious? Ha! I didn't think so. This type of goodness—this level of magnificence and splendor—is not yet something we know how to measure. Even with all of our current striving, it still isn't something that we could achieve for ourselves. Thank you, Estée Lauder, but no. I'll let the Lord, not your cosmetic line, define my worth and beauty.

Our culture values women who are nice to look at. Women who are independent, confident, ambitious. We forget that, biblically, a woman is also honored for being gentle, with a quiet spirit (1 Pet. 3:4); for being wise, hardworking, generous, God-fearing, and yes, trustworthy (Prov. 31:10–31). So, we strive to be perfect and popular. Often without second thought, we compromise our values to get there, because it's what "everyone else is doing." But this isn't who we are, who God made us to be.

In the Sermon on the Mount, historically one of the most quoted sections of Scripture, Jesus describes the distinctive qualities of a citizen of heaven, someone who has received the promise of eternal life and reveres God's everlasting light. Oddly enough, the traits have absolutely nothing to do with being able-bodied or attractive. They also don't mention being financially well-off or a member of an exclusive organization. Or is that really a coincidence at all?

Meager — Able to recognize you have nothing apart from God; totally dependent on him.

Sorrowful — Willing to acknowledge the extent of your sin and shortcomings. Able to admit you'll never be worthy.

Meek — Capable of practicing self-control in accordance with God's will. Has a divine perspective; suffers strong.

Doesn't seek power, possessions, pleasure, but holiness, righteousness. Has a "longing for heaven that endures." — **Hungry**

Able to show compassion. Willing to restore what's broken. — **Big-hearted**

Has integrity; is obedient. Able to give undivided attention + wholehearted devotion to the Lord. — **Pure-hearted**

Peacemaker — Stops all that isn't holy or pleasing to the Lord; able to focus on what is true, noble, right, pure, holy, admirable . . .

Persecuted — Willing to suffer in obedience; a true friend of Christ.

Write these on your heart, friend, so you can walk forward in faith, focused not on the expectations you were once trying to meet but, rather, on the characteristics you already possess as citizen of heaven (Phil. 3:20).

You belong to God (Eph. 1:13, 1:5–6). You are his child (John 1:12), his friend (John 15:15). You are his masterpiece (Eph. 2:10). You are made holy (1 Cor. 1:2, 1:30; Eph. 1:4). No amount of invitations, awards, or accolades will ever top the truth your heart already holds. We only have so much time, a finite number of days on this Earth. We don't want to waste it by trying to figure out who we are when God has already told us. Find your purpose and fulfill it.

When Esther married King Xerxes, she became queen of the Persian Empire. Can you imagine being thrust into such a luxurious lifestyle? I hate to admit it, but I would probably love having a stylist, a personal trainer, a nutritionist, a maid. Chances are I would be thrilled to pick out fine china and table settings, hors d'oeuvres and fancy champagne. Yet, regardless of Esther's title, she is mentioned, biblically, for her faithfulness, for her ability to realize that her resources and her place in history were planned by God, for a purpose. Where you live and what you own may not be as coincidental as you might think. Your blessings? Not just for you. Find the reason for them, and act accordingly.

Who knows? The Christian influencers, the sorority women, the members of the Junior League who seemingly "have it all" may give an incredible amount of their resources to God. Yet, to me, it looks like they have more to give. We all do. We're expected to give in accordance with what we've been given (2 Cor. 8:12). For example, if you can afford to serve the Lord well *and* live in a fancy home, it doesn't mean you should. If you're serving him in accordance, you'd never be able to afford a fancy home in the first place. Regardless of the size of their income, do you think it's appropriate, for a Christian, to drive a Mercedes, wear Tom Ford sunglasses, or fly first class? I'm not sure how you answered this question, but here's another for you: Shouldn't we, as Christians, be dumping our resources back out into the world, for Jesus, just as fast as we receive them?

— *Questions* —

1. "For our God is a devouring fire" (Heb. 12:29 NLT). If everything sinful and worthless were devoured by his wrath, would anything in your life be left?

2. If you're obsessing over makeup, if you're consumed by Greek letters, if you're misusing your God-given resources, then you're trying to be a friend of the world while trying to be a friend of God. And biblically, we're told we can't have both. James 4:4 (NLT): "You adulterers! Don't you realize that friendship with the world makes you an enemy of God?"

3. Have you done anything recently that has made you a friend and imitator of the world?

4. Have you done anything recently that has made you a friend and imitator of Christ?

Prayer

Father God, it's easy to get sucked into all the world offers. Free me from its grip, from the standard it imposes. There will be times I wish I could drive luxury cars and join elite organizations, but in these moments, remind me who I am in you. Make me brave, make me bold. Make me a leader. I'm deciding, in this moment, that you matter more. Thank you for laying this foundation for me. Thank you for showing me that this space of "satisfaction" is not where I was meant to be.

NOTES

[1] George Barna, *The Seven Faith Tribes: Who They Are, What They Believe, and Why They Matter* (Carol Stream, IL: Tyndale, 2009).

[2] "Self-Described Christians Dominate America but Wrestle with Four Aspects of Spiritual Depth," *Barna*, September 13, 2011, https://www.barna.com/research/self-described-christians-dominate-america-but-wrestle-with-four-aspects-of-spiritual-depth/.

[3] John Piper, *What Is Saving Faith? Reflections on Receiving Christ as a Treasure* (Wheaton, IL: Crossway, 2022), 29.

[4] Jia Tolentino, "Athleisure, Barre and Kale," *The Guardian*, August 2, 2019, www.theguardian.com/news/2019/aug/02/athleisure-barre-kale-tyranny-ideal-woman-labour.

[5] *Keeping Up with the Kardashians*, aired from 2007 to 2021 on E!

[6] Jill Lawrence, "Junior League Battles Elitist Image," *Los Angeles Times*, June 24, 1990, https://www.latimes.com/archives/la-xpm-1990-06-24-mn-621-story.html.

[7] Prudence Mackintosh, "My Life and Hard Times in the Junior League," *Texas Monthly*, December 1979, https://www.texasmonthly.com/being-texan/my-life-and-hard-times-in-the-junior-league/.

[8] Kate Garrett, "Southern Sororities Have a Jesus Problem," *Kate's Journal* (blog), https://www.kates-journal.com/writing-samples/southern-sororities-have-a-jesus-problem.

[9] Lawrence, "Junior League Battles Elitist Image."

SEVEN

Reinventing the American Dream

Graduate from high school. Go to college. Get your dream job. Get married. Make money. Buy a house. Get a dog. Buy a car. Have a kid. Raise the kid. Send the kid to college. Retire. Die? It's easy to get caught up in the American dream, even if on paper it seems kind of depressing.

For generations, Americans have measured their success based on standards that emphasize wealth, material possessions, and power. But, beyond fleeting comfort and a false sense of security, what do these standards really offer? Are they a source of peace? Do they bring authentic joy? Or are they simply idols we chase because it's "the normal thing to do"?

We're stuck in a cycle that vows to make us prosperous, so we spend most of our time and energy pursuing things that are totally unrelated to what satisfies our souls and propels us forward in obedience to God. And before we know it, we're too tied down by our belongings and secular responsibilities to fully realize our purpose here, which is to be an asset to his kingdom.

But here's the good news: the God who spoke the world into existence is the same God who knit you together in your mother's womb, who laid out every moment of your life before it began. Even then, he knew you intimately, and although he saw your sin, self-righteousness, and shortcomings, he still traded his life for yours. Is this not the best thing ever? It frees us from so much.

In his presence, our strivings cease. We let go of earthly demands and expectations. We still the chaos and step away from the hustle. Because somewhere deep in our hearts, we know that our proximity to Jesus isn't based on our job title, wealth, social status, or anything else.

In each new season, I encourage you to sit down with a journal and sort through the details of your life so you're able to tell what your heart's really after, where you're really storing your treasure. It's difficult to be part of a society and *not* adopt its expectation and instruction. We often do so subconsciously, and God knows this. How do we move forward when our already established lives are buried deep within the confines of the American dream? How do we shift our permanent perspective from earthly to eternal?

Swap Out the Soil

Look at your life. What do you value? Your career? Your family? If what matters to you the most doesn't have Jesus written all over it, you may have built your house on a weak foundation. But it's not too late, friend! You can move! To be a faithful, trustworthy asset to his kingdom, you must build your life on solid rock: Jesus and his teachings. In fact, we're not just called to listen to him, but to base our lives on his principles and promises (James 1:22).

When my husband and I were building a house in the Florida panhandle, I jokingly panicked about it being built on sandy soil. In fact, if I remember correctly, we were even encouraged to purchase sinkhole insurance, because sometimes sand really does prove itself to be an insufficient foundation. And a sinkhole, by definition, is an "internal void or cavity" often caused by shifting or eroding sand.[1] I remember when this was being explained to us, I wanted to laugh out loud at the absurdity of it all. Was it a coincidence that Jesus used this exact example in the New Testament to illustrate the fate of a foolish man, one who hears God's Word and does not build his life on it (Matt. 7:24–27)? Although we were physically—not spiritually—laying a foundation across a quarter-acre of sand, I still felt the weight of the risk. You'd be happy to know that we've lived here almost four years now and the foundation has yet to cave in. Be that as it may, it doesn't minimize the potential danger of a hole in the earth around or beneath our home—the damage would be catastrophic. What do you think happens to a heart when it, too, is set on a weak foundation? The shifting winds of life just might cause the foundation to weaken—one grain at a time—and before we know it, there's an internal void, a cavity, causing the structure to fall. What's even more dangerous? Sinkholes can take years to form, and they do so underground, undetected. It's possible to move in and out of a house without ever realizing what's happening right below you. Faith works the same way. We can live a life that (we think) is built on a good foundation when really it isn't. We can trick ourselves, especially when we're living in a "satisfied" space, into believing that we *are* followers of Christ. And some of us will live and die before we realize that the foundation we laid wasn't built on solid ground, on the one real truth, on God.

Not only does your foundation matter, but the integrity of the builder is extremely important. Psalm 127:1 tells us that unless the Lord builds a house, the work of the builder is wasted. This signifies that we have the capacity to build a life on our own, a life that seems good, enjoyable, God-honoring. But if our foundation isn't assembled based on the promises of God, and if God himself isn't the one doing the building, then our work is not only fruitless but trivial. Nevertheless, we spend an enormous amount of time trying to make our own way. Remember who you are—that you are you and God is God. God is the foundation. God is the architect, the builder, everything. We must realize our place before we're able to realize our purpose.

Remember There Is More

God did not dream you up in his heart and create you in his hands just so you could be verified on Instagram or afford to send your kids to private school. These might be the realities we hope for, but God intends for us to hope bigger, to hope deeper, to hope in proximity to him. Jesus declares in the New Testament that he came to "give [us] a rich and satisfying life" (John 10:10 NLT). Yet, we've proven ourselves to be too small-minded, too worldly, to realize that Jesus isn't talking about material wealth or temporal pleasure. He's not claiming to have died for us so we can "live our best life" or achieve the American dream. He's stating that he came so we may experience a life in Christ *here* and in heaven, the chance to know him *and* spend eternity with him. Everything else is like chasing the wind (Eccles. 1:14). Even still, the wind is what we're after.

While we can appreciate, to an extent, what he did for us by securing eternity, I don't think we're able to truly fathom all that awaits. We naturally can't see past our present circumstances, and this can be overwhelming and distressing. We're promised a perfect life in heaven, but we try to make *this* life the one that's rich and satisfying and complete. We marvel at our surroundings like they're even comparable to what's yet to be revealed. When I try to think about what eternity looks like, I just want to go outside and scream it from my driveway. I want to cheer loudly, dance, run sprints—the joy isn't containable; it bursts from within me. We're promised a place that Jesus refers to as "paradise" (Luke 23:43 NLT); a place where there will be no death, no mourning, no crying, no pain (Rev. 21:4); a place whose glory far outweighs our present sufferings (Rom. 8:18); a place where glory is beyond all comparison (2 Cor. 4:17); a place where there is "joy in the presence of angels" (Luke 15:10 AMP); with all nations, tribes and peoples and languages (Rev. 7:9); a place where even a day is better than a thousand spent elsewhere (Ps. 84:10). The dwelling place of the Lord, a holy habitation (Deut. 26:15). Just by reminding ourselves, reminding each other, that there is *more*, we can shift our perspective, our hopes, our dreams, our desires, from a hopeful present to a hopeful future, a hopeful end.

Listen for Him

I'm not suggesting the clouds will part and a coffee order will rain down upon you when you're being indecisive in the drive-thru line. Order what you want, and make it snappy—there are people behind you. What I am suggesting, however, is that sometimes God uses a basic situation—such as your time in the drive-thru line—to capture your attention and ultimately change your life. Work on slowing down, on being still. Search for him even in the moments that seem ordinary and inconspicuous.

Moses was herding sheep. Job was hanging out with friends. Solomon was sleeping. Elijah was camping. When God speaks, it isn't loud or chaotic. He isn't only heard on the mountaintops but in the valleys, in the stillness, in the whisper of the wind (1 Kings 19:11–13). It's difficult *not* to be preoccupied with our jobs, our growing families, our secular obligations, but our hearts must remain unoccupied in the chaos, or we'll have made it easy to miss God.

Give It All to God

First Peter 5:7 (NLT) tells us to "give all [our] worries and cares to God." Why? Because he cares about what we care about! To "pray without ceasing" (1 Thess. 5:17 ESV) means we take our fears and failures to him, but also our joy, gratitude, hope, and everything in between. We often think that God doesn't care about the lesser details of our lives, but as a father who deeply loves his children, he wants to be part of it all.

Has anyone ever told you to "Let go and let God"? I've always considered this to be a poor and overused response to a season of suffering or waiting. Yet in reality, it's great advice. When you physically hand something to someone else—let's say, a piece of paper—the paper is taken from your hands and you no longer possess it. Letting things go, in the presence of God, should be just as permanent. When you place your circumstances at the feet of Jesus, they are moving from your hands to his. You're passing them off, no longer possessing them. God wants us to do this with everything, all the time. He wants us to surrender the unknown, the things we aren't yet able to understand, but he also wants us to hand him our careers even if they're incredible, our finances even if they're stable, our marriages even if they're making it. Are there areas of your life you're unwilling to hand over? Maybe you've given your children to God because you realize that they were never really yours to begin with, but maybe you haven't yet offered him your cushy job, too. Don't run the risk of being ineffective, unproductive, or ultimately unworthy of the work of God because you're not willing to surrender it all.

Practice Grace and Patience

His plans and timing are different from our own, and believe it or not, this is a good thing. His provision is endless. His protection is constant. And he points us in the right direction when he knows we're ready. A season of waiting *on* him is just a season of trusting *in* him. What a miraculous blessing it is that he's the one we get to wait for. If we are actively seeking him and participating in his will, he will work all things for our good (and his glory) while we rest, worship, and prepare. Although we don't like to wait, this is actually a pretty sweet spot to be in because we are being held by God. Noah waited for almost a year (Gen. 8:1–17). Joseph waited two (Gen. 40–41). Abraham waited twenty-five (Gen. 12–21). Caleb waited forty-five (Josh. 14:6–15). Even God waits on us for long periods of time.

The Bible tells us to ask and it will be given, to seek and it will be found, to knock and it will be opened (Matt. 7:7–8). Yet, it doesn't imply that these things happen immediately or in ways we expect or understand. We must learn to wait well and in a manner that's pleasing to the Lord. Psalms 27:14 (NLT) encourages us to "wait patiently for the LORD."

Focus on His People

We're usually too busy building a life to realize it's the people we're building it with—a sibling, spouse, best friend, roommate, coworker—who are the most important. Whoever your people are in this season, love them well, pray with them often, and walk them toward Jesus like it's the whole point of your purpose here. Because, well, it might be.

Most generally, even as the self-proclaimed "hands and feet" (Matt. 22:13 NLT) of Jesus, we willingly address our neighbors' needs until our finances and comfortability tell us otherwise. Our response to someone's pain, sickness, long-suffering, or wandering is often not what God intended it to be. We show up, but we don't stay long. We have more important things to do, our own problems to deal with. We cross the street because we're inconvenienced. We look the other way because we're fearful. We brush it off because we're unsure.

Now would probably be a good time to admit that I've never shared the gospel with a stranger. I've never talked about Jesus with an agnostic friend or atheist family member. I've never invited anyone to church. Why do I so casually keep him to myself? Is it because of our nation's political climate? Or because doing so is considered a social faux pas? Whatever the reason, I have an obligation, as a child of God, as a part of his hands and feet, to bring others with me to heaven. The truth is, I should want this more than anything. God says that those who love him don't show up empty-handed (Exod. 23:15), but in this case, I nearly would be.

If God were at the very center of our existence, we would be too busy producing fruit to wonder if we were or not. We wouldn't enter his presence without the best of everything we had—true offerings. We have to stop assuming that we'll have time later to invite someone to church, share the gospel, offer our best to God. One day, we'll be wrong about this. It will suddenly no longer be a "future us" problem. We'll lose touch with the friend who wasn't a believer. A sudden, tragic accident will rob us of the opportunity to show our neighbor the light of life. Or we'll find ourselves standing before him as empty-handed as we were when he first created us, with nothing that proves our lives were lived for him. In that moment, do you think we'll be able to feel the regret, the weight, of all we didn't do while we had the chance? As followers of Christ, our hearts should be overflowing with the Holy Spirit. Living water should spill out and splash onto the people in our proximity. If this isn't how we're carrying ourselves, we need to reevaluate the way we love his people and, ultimately, the way we love Jesus.

Live in the Word

Yesterday, I heard a woman talking about her extremely busy life. Between working full-time and having three young kids, she said she always feels rushed, like there aren't enough hours in the day.

Not even for her closest friends. I wondered if Jesus was included in that category, because that's what happens to us. We become so preoccupied with secular responsibilities that we fail to make time for what really matters: Jesus's people and Jesus himself.

Pastors often stress the importance of getting alone with God, even for five minutes if that's all the time you have. Do they mean the leftover five minutes? Because that's often what it becomes. The time we spend with Jesus, in his Word and at his feet, should be what everything else is centered around. Instead, we build our schedule and try to fit him in when and if we can, often forgetting that the book we leave sitting on our shelves, nightstands, and floor is actually the written Word of God. It is a love letter meant to draw us near(er). It is a manual to help us restore our priorities and live for Jesus.

I don't know much about college football, but I do know that Mark Richt was the head coach at the University of Georgia while my older sister was living in Athens, Georgia. While he's known for the success of his football programs, what really caught my attention was the way he demonstrates his faith. In his book, *Make the Call*, he discusses the weight of constant decision-making, whether on the field or in everyday life. "Sometimes," he says, "you have time to decide; you have days, hours—you have a chance to hear from God. But, other times, you have to make the call in that moment based on your preparation, the time you spent with the Lord. So, when you do make a fast decision, hopefully it's one that's in line with what God would have you do."[2]

Whether you're coaching, working, or parenting, life is full of split-second decisions, some harder than others. Do you want a cappuccino or a latte? Do you yell at your child in anger or wait two minutes for your emotions to regulate? Do you mention Jesus to the stranger next to you, or do you put your headphones in and decide it isn't a good time? If you haven't prepared well, how will you know what decision to make? Will you be too paralyzed to make one at all? The time we spend in God's Word is sometimes all we have. So, we must prepare wisely. Remaining close to the Lord will lay the groundwork for how we act, react, speak, steward, teach, and choose in each moment. And these moments, if we do them well, will bring joy to the Lord by producing fruit in our lives.

God's call to Joshua after Moses's death? Read the Word, speak the Word, think about the Word, do what the Word says (Josh. 1:6–9). Even now, this is what it means to follow God. In the movie *Miss Congeniality*, Michael Caine mouths to Sandra Bullock while she's on the Miss America stage, "Wear the crown. Be the crown. You are the crown!"[3] I will never not quote this movie—it is just so, so good. This is the attitude we should have toward Jesus too—eat, sleep, live the Word.

Use Each Resource Responsibly

The first time I heard my husband say the word *budget*, I immediately began to feel cold and empty inside. I think I even asked him for an example so I could better understand just how much my life was about to change. While I agreed with him that a spending plan is responsible and adult(ish), I hated it at first. For obvious reasons, budgets aren't fun. They tell you to put "it" back; we aren't getting "it" today. They tell you that, unfortunately, you'll have to wait to get "it" or miss out on "it" altogether. But even while I internally pouted, I took responsibility by making the budget somewhat of a game, a personal challenge. I genuinely tried not to overspend, but when you're a bored housewife with a kid, that's sometimes hard to do, you know what I mean? Luckily, my husband had set money aside so we wouldn't be in a bind when I failed. Because he knew I would fail. (By the way, I'm mainly talking about the way *I* spend money because my husband hasn't bought anything of note since June of last year and my son is still too young to know how to shop online.)

Six months into our money tracking, and I was hating it even more than I originally thought possible. Not only was it hindering me, but it also had the audacity to publicize all the ways in which I was wasting our income. A few large coffees, a couple new outfits, plants I kept killing and rebuying. Honestly, I was both stunned and embarrassed. Before the budget, we would get to the end of a pay period and question where our money had gone. Our lives moved at such a fast pace it had become easy to spend money at an impossible rate.

I started to realize that budgets are, as much as I hate them, a healthy way not only to save money but to hold yourself accountable. And this matters because the money isn't really ours in the first place—it belongs to God. As does every blessing we receive this side of eternity (James 1:17). When my soul was able to fully recognize this and learn to use our resources accordingly, a budget was a welcomed incrimination. Now, I'm thankful we have a tool that helps us process our God-given resources so we can use them in a way that's pleasing to the Lord, not just pleasing to ourselves. Our time here isn't about collecting resources anyway but using our resources to collect people (Matt. 4:19).

If you're the "breadwinner" in your home or have worked hard to get where you are, you may feel like you earned the money yourself. In reality, God provided everything required to earn it in the first place: ability, creativity, intelligence, motivation. In John 15, Jesus teaches that, apart from him, we can do nothing. He isn't only talking about miracle work; he's literally telling us that without him, we can do *no thing*. This alone should make us want to change the way we selfishly use our resources. We should be giving the best of everything back to God and doing so joyfully.

We might sit on our deathbed and regret the vacations we didn't take, the promotions we never received, the weight we didn't lose, but we won't be thinking about any of that when we stand before God mere moments later. Any success associated with the American dream ends at death's doorway. The best part about living your life for Jesus? It truly begins at the doorstep of eternity.

— *Questions* —

1. What does "reinventing" the American dream look like for you in your own life?

2. How will you ensure you're able to make these changes permanently?

Prayer

Father, help the American dream lose its appeal. It is but a smokescreen, ultimately barring me from the purpose you've placed on my life. Please remind me that, in each moment, you offer more joy, long(er)-lasting comfort, and peace beyond comprehension.

NOTES

[1] "What Is a Sinkhole?," US Geological Survey, https://www.usgs.gov/faqs/what-a-sinkhole.

[2] Mark Richt, *Make the Call: Game-Day Wisdom for Life's Defining Moments* (Nashville: B&H, 2021).

[3] *Miss Congeniality*, directed by Donald Petrie (Burbank, CA: Warner Bros. Pictures, 2000).

EIGHT

Obedience before _____

Our feminist culture is outraged by biblical womanhood. It's not comfortable with what it means to be obedient. It's offended by the concept of submission. In fact, yielding to any kind of authority is frowned upon because, honey, "You don't need no man." And unfortunately, sometimes, that includes Jesus. But if you've spent time in a healthy, Christ-honoring church, you know that obedience and submission not only help define our roles in the kingdom but our expected behavior as followers of Christ. John 3:16, easily one of the most recognized verses in the New Testament, says that "whoever believes in him shall not perish but have eternal life" (NIV). However, twenty verses later, it also states that those who believe but do not obey will never experience it (John 3:36). You can believe God is real but not know him intimately. You can profess with your mouth but not trust with your heart. You can follow him but not be obedient.

In the book of Matthew, Jesus uses a story of two sons to illustrate those who have an outward expression of faith but never truly obey God. The first son, when asked by his father to go help in the vineyard, initially says no. Then, once he realizes he's been disobedient, he goes to the vineyard to work. The second son immediately says yes but never actually steps foot on the estate. Maybe he lied, never planning to go; maybe he had good intentions but never followed through (Matt. 21:28–32). Words and promises are not enough. "I meant well" doesn't matter.

Countless American Christians have accepted Christ, professed their faith publicly, and been baptized, but then have gone back to living the way they did before—and our culture largely accepts this. Sometimes the heart change is drastic. Someone meets Jesus and stops abusing drugs, watching porn, cheating on their spouse. But other times, the inward shift is more subtle, calling forth no real change of everyday patterns or behaviors. The sin may not be obvious but rather so deeply embedded within that person, so normalized, that it's easy for them to miss it—materialism, hedonism, idolism. When the transformation of soul and spirit doesn't seem monumental or permanent, it isn't taken seriously. And inevitably, obedience to the Lord isn't, either.

The Bible, however, makes it clear: when we make the decision to follow Christ, we are called to act like it. Peter challenged the churches in exile to live holy, obedient lives. "So, you must live as God's obedient children. Don't slip back into your old ways of living to satisfy your own desires. You didn't know any better then. But now you must be holy in everything you do, just as God who chose you is holy" (1 Pet. 1:14–16 NLT). God may do the transforming, but we must accept and uphold it. After all, we are responsible for the truth that we know. "To whom much has been given, much will be required" (Luke 12:48 AMP). We often refer to this verse when talking about physical or financial blessings. Yet, doesn't it also apply to our knowledge of the gospel and our relationship with Jesus?

We can't be obedient in our calling if we don't first obey the Lord's most basic teachings. If you grew up like a typical church kid, you can most likely recite the Ten Commandments in order of which they were presented to the covenant community. While I'm sure your Sunday school teacher would be proud, this might actually not do any favors for you. At times, it's evident that because of our rote memorization of them, we obey the commandments exclusively as they're stated in the Old Testament. We don't steal, we don't kill, but we also don't look beyond the face value of these commands. We forget Jesus's full explanation of them in the New Testament. This, of course, is not only negligent, but it endangers our ability to be obedient. Let's take a closer look:

> **"You must not have any other god but me"** (Exod. 20:3 NLT). You shouldn't be preoccupied with anything in all of creation, except for the creator himself. But I know that even in your constant pursuit of Jesus, there is, in all likelihood, other things that occupy your mind. The last time I binge-watched a TV series, it was all I could think about for days. I replayed the scenes in my head over and over again while driving, jogging, blow-drying my hair. I would rush through my day just so I could spare a couple of hours for the newest episode. I was consumed by mindless entertainment and detached from reality. This is idolatry.

"You must not make yourself an idol of any kind or an image of anything in the heavens or on the earth or in the sea" (Exod. 20:4–5 NLT). In the ancient world, there were gods for everything—fate, fortune, fertility—and after God rescued the Israelites from Egyptian slavery, he demanded that this be changed. You may look at this commandment and think, "Great, I'm obedient! I don't pray to anyone else or have little wooden people scattered around my house." But this commandment actually overlaps the first one, as its primary focus is idolatry: whom we worship and how.

"You must not misuse the name of the Lord your God" (Exod. 20:7 NLT). According to David Guzik, one of the most popular Bible commentators of our age, this command is disobeyed when one uses the name of God to curse, blaspheme, or "[act] in a way that disgraces Him."[1] Despite its prevalence in our culture and our Christian circles, I've trained myself not to say, "Oh my God!" Even the Amazon box I received in the mail last week had "Oh. My. God [. . .] Look. At. This. Box." printed on the side. The words might not mean anything to your heart, but if your lips continuously speak them, your flippant attitude toward the Lord will seep into other areas of your life. Maybe you think you're off the hook because, like me, you choose not to speak this way. However, the commandment also forbids us from dishonoring God. If we associate with his name while gossiping, complaining, or misusing his resources, we disgrace him greatly. And as Christian women, we are guilty of this.

"Remember to observe the Sabbath day by keeping it holy" (Exod. 20:8 NLT). If so far you've claimed you aren't a sinner, this commandment will make you one. The very basis of the American dream is hard, nonstop work—workaholism. As a matter of fact, the days we aren't working at an office are usually spent working at home doing laundry, mowing the yard, and prepping for the week ahead. Rest, in our culture, is a sign of laziness and ineptitude. Yet, while God was busy creating the whole world, he still found a day to rest. Arguably, this commandment isn't demanding a day of idleness, but it is stipulating an acknowledgment of not only our ability to rest but the luxury we have to do so because of the salvation work he's already completed. Whatever our theories are on this, we're probably still spending too much time working on secular things and not enough time observing his holiness and allowing our body and mind to rest in his presence.

"Honor your father and mother" (Exod. 20:12 NLT). Even if they're estranged, altogether absent, or abusive, God commands us to respect our parents in words and behaviors. God could very well be requesting harmonious relationships between age groups in the larger culture as well. Older generations tend to think that younger people are lost and lazy; younger generations think that older people are irrelevant and out of touch. This creates a division in and outside of the church that Satan, sooner or later, uses for his purposes.

"You must not murder" (Exod. 20:13 NLT). I can't help you with this one, sister. If there's a body in your backyard, you're on your own. Yet even though the sixth commandment seems straightforward, it isn't so easily defined. When Jesus says "thou shalt not kill," he is also banning hatred. If you've ever told anyone they're "dead" to you, it's kind of the same thing in the eyes of the Lord. "You have heard that our ancestors were told, 'you must not murder. If you commit murder, you are subject to judgment.' But I say, if you are even angry with someone, you are subject to judgment! If you call someone an idiot, you are in danger of being brought before the court. And if you curse someone, you are in danger of the fires of hell" (Matt. 5:21–22 NLT).

"You must not commit adultery" (Exod. 20:14 NLT). Extramarital sex is a sin—end of story. However, Jesus also claims that adultery is committed in our hearts just by lusting after someone (Matt. 5:27). I was scrolling on social media last week (be careful, I know!) and saw a picture of one of my favorite country music stars. The first comment? "I'm married, but it's not that serious." While I knew it was a joke, I also felt it exposed the woman's inner thoughts. Maybe in a different setting she would also claim to be a follower of Christ. I guess I'll never know the state of her heart when she posted the comment, but I'm responsible for the state of mine. And I know I not only want to honor my husband, but I also want to honor God.

"You must not steal" (Exod. 20:15 NLT). The last time I took something from a store that I didn't pay for, I was a two-year-old child in a stroller. After my mom noticed I was chewing on a bottle of nail polish, she returned it to the store on my behalf. So, I'm technically good, right? Wrong. I steal from the Lord each time I'm blatantly disobedient, each time I keep the gospel to myself, each time I squander the resources he has given.

"You must not testify falsely against your neighbor" (Exod. 20:16 NLT). If you've ever been to court, I hope you didn't lie on the stand. But once again, we have ourselves a commandment that is multisided. Gossiping, lying, or even remaining silent in some situations can make you disobedient to the ninth commandment. I was hopeful that, by my late twenties, I would've grown out of this schoolgirl mentality. I've noticed, however, that a lot of women never do. Even Christian ones.

"You must not covet your neighbor's house. You must not covet your neighbor's wife, male or female servant, ox or donkey, or anything else that belongs to your neighbor" (Exod. 20:17 NLT). I'm sure you've never wanted your neighbor's livestock, but have you ever looked at their car, their home gym, their successful kid, and thought, "Boy, I'd like to have one of those?" In a sense, the Lord is commanding us to be satisfied with what he's given—anything less opens the door to idolatry.

Obedience also includes making disciples of all nations (Matt. 28:19), being fruitful and multiplying (Gen. 1:28), and loving your enemies (Matt. 5:44). Obedience is acknowledging the sovereignty of God, that his will and his ways are higher than your own (Isa. 55:8–9). Obedience looks like enduring malfeasance (Matt. 5:38–42); giving, praying, and fasting privately (Matt. 6:1–18); not worrying (Phil. 4:6); not judging others (Matt. 7:1–5). Are you exhausted yet? There's so much to obey but so much hope offered in Christ. If you remain in his presence and focus on his purpose, he'll guide your heart toward truth and honor, toward what is right and pure and lovely, toward things that are admirable and excellent and worthy of praise (Phil. 4:8). And you'll be well on your way to obedience. This is the part where we step into the presence of God and ask for help.

Even still, obedience might seem a bit convoluted. There's obvious obedience and there's deliberate disobedience but, as I mentioned earlier, there are also myriad responses found in-between. All of them are worth thinking about because how we choose to be obedient matters to God as much as the result of our obedience.

Hard-hearted disobedience. Most likely, there are people in your life who are happy to be agnostic or atheistic. People who, because of their self-sufficiency or self-absorption, don't want to know God or don't think they would benefit from a relationship with him. Yet, choosing not to recognize or submit to his will doesn't take them out of the running, nor does it make them exempt from the reality of hell. It only makes them disobedient. And unfortunately, after so many attempts, God may let them go their own way and allow their hearts to harden. Paul referenced this in his letter to the Roman church. "Since they thought it foolish to acknowledge God, he abandoned them to their foolish thinking and let them do things that should never be done" (Rom. 1:28 NLT). We see this exemplified, really for the first time, in Exodus. After Moses and Aaron visited Pharoah to request the release of God's people, Pharoah answered, "Who is the LORD? Why should I listen to him and let Israel go? I don't know the LORD, and I will not let Israel go" (Exod. 5:2 NLT). Pharoah's heart wasn't hardened against his own will. He, without reserve, didn't want to know God and proved to be unresponsive, untrustworthy, and unmoving.

"I meant well" disobedience. This is typically the response of a casual Christian (I'm speaking from experience here), or, in other words, someone who interprets the gospel to fit their needs, based on how it relates to their culture, their family, or even their personal "truth." Unsurprisingly, this causes disobedience. If your foundation is weak, or if you're lost, distracted, or self-focused, you run the risk of being well-intentioned but not obedient. At the end of your life, there won't be an excuse for this.

Matthew 7:13–14 (NLT) says, "You can enter God's Kingdom only through the narrow gate. The highway to hell is broad, and its gate is wide for the many who choose that way. But the gateway to life is very narrow and the road is difficult, and only a few ever find it." This reminds me of the phrase, "The road to hell is paved with good intentions." I've also recently heard someone say, "Hell is full of good planning, but heaven is full of good works." If you're someone who doesn't follow through in secular situations and relationships, it's time to examine your relationship with the Lord to ensure you aren't also treating him this way. I'm sure he values your good intentions, but at what point are good intentions no longer enough?

Blatant disobedience. Adam and Eve ate the fruit (Gen. 3:1–6). Lot's wife looked back (Gen. 19:1–26). Ananias and Sapphira lied and withheld (Acts 5:1–10). Sometimes we choose disobedience because we're scared, tempted, or just don't know how to listen and faithfully follow through. Regardless of the reason, this is the type of defiance that threatens our souls. Hebrews 10:26 (NLT) says, "If we deliberately continue sinning after we have received knowledge of the truth, there is no longer any sacrifice that will cover these sins."

Delayed obedience. Occasionally, after we blatantly disobey God, we circle back, fully aware we missed an opportunity to walk in obedience. We learn from our mistakes and open our hearts to submission, even if at first we were off to a rough start. Remember Jonah and the whale? It was my favorite Bible story as a child. Yet, all I really knew was that Jonah was ingested by a fish and didn't die. I hadn't given much thought as to why God had allowed it.

As it turns out, Jonah was swallowed because when God asked him to go to Nineveh, he chose to go in the opposite direction to "escape from the presence of the LORD" (Jon. 1:3 AMP). How's that for blatant disobedience? While Jonah may have been rebellious, God didn't abandon him in that place. He gave him a chance to circle back and be obedient. Jonah 3:3 (NLT) says, "This time, Jonah obeyed the LORD's command and went to Nineveh." Our God is a god of second chances, yet we can't assume he'll always give us one. Our obedience must be careful and immediate.

Selective obedience. When Saul and his army were given instructions from the Lord, they essentially went through and picked which parts they were going to obey. They were told to destroy everything completely, yet they decided to spare and save for themselves the best of what was left (1 Sam. 15:9). Casual Christians, me included, often mistake this for obedience. Yet, no matter how you swing it, it's not. "For the person who keeps all of the laws except one is as guilty as a person who has broken all of God's laws" (James 2:10 NLT).

Half-hearted obedience. Hi, it's me again—the casual Christian. I seem to be super into types of obedience that aren't really obedience at all. I tithe but don't always do so cheerfully. I help friends but sometimes do so out of guilt. I follow God into the unknown but often do so reluctantly. Why have I allowed myself to become so apathetic, so inconvenienced by obedience? Second Chronicles 25:2 (NLT) says, "Amaziah did what was pleasing in the LORD's sight, but not wholeheartedly." Why did Ezra feel the need to mention that Amaziah obeyed but did so half-heartedly? Well, because it's just that important. While we aren't given much detail, we are told about the condition of his heart and his partial surrender. This isn't how we're called to live as children of God.

Careful obedience. This is what we should be working toward—the wisdom and preparation to discern what God is asking and the intentionality to follow through. This usually requires us to be still and silent before the Lord. Remember, he often whispers. We don't want to flippantly obey or "wing it." We want to not only take it seriously but to do it in a manner that pleases the Lord. Like Abraham sacrificing Isaac (Gen. 22)—blind, immediate obedience. Sometimes I feel like I'm bouncing around aimlessly because I've missed or subconsciously ignored my purpose. But what I do understand is this: God is sovereign, and if you seek him with all your heart, you *will* find him. He will direct your steps. He will teach you what it means to be obedient—willingly, cheerfully, blindly obedient.

Although it may seem like it, your pursuit of holiness is not a game to God. He wants your heart, your commitment. He wants you to seek him, yes, but he also wants to be found. It's important to note, however, that even after you've surrendered and stepped into your life purpose, it won't make his will always that much clearer. We're never, at any point in our faith walk, given a blueprint or step-by-step process on how to be obedient. While the Bible is an irreplaceable resource and will be significantly helpful to you, there will come a time when you're forced to step into faith, allowing God alone to guide you, hold you, fulfill you. It's truly like you're blind, and faith is the only way to take the next step forward. I have "walk by faith" from 2 Corinthians 5:7 (AMP) tattooed on my right foot because once I understood the concept, I knew it was something I couldn't afford to miss. The verse not only says "Walk by faith" but goes as far to include "not by sight." The emphasis here is on the latter. Maybe we're supposed to walk not by sight but by faith because what we see distracts us. What we see keeps us from being fully reliant and blindly obedient.

Obedience before Understanding

The ability to understand and be understood is classified as a fundamental human need.[2] We have an internal drive to explore and explain, to make sense of what's around us. And I don't think the trait is accidental. I do, however, think we've taken it a bit too far. We don't usually accept the things we can't understand, and because of this, people either don't believe in God or they're indifferent about him. Following, trusting, and obeying would require an uncomfortable, unrealistic amount of acceptance in exchange for an explanation that is severely lacking. We always want to fully understand each detail before we sign on the dotted line, but that's not what faith is, is it? Biblically, we're told that faith is "the assurance of things hoped for, the conviction of things not seen" (Heb. 11:1 ESV). Secularly, faith is defined as "belief in God or in the doctrines or teachings of religion," or "belief that is not based on proof."[3] Although both versions mention partial understanding, they also mention a level of belief that isn't hindered by it. Most people aren't innately interested in moving forward if they aren't sure where they're going to end up, but that's what faith asks us to do.

Sometimes, I'm okay with not having all the answers. I find a way to move forward with peace, acknowledging that God is perfectly capable of holding my life in his hands. But other times, I find myself losing sleep over the anxiety of not knowing what the future holds. I beg God for a sign, a glimpse, anything, and when he doesn't provide it, I sometimes feel more discouraged, more confused, and of course, ashamed about my lack of faith and obedience. What helps me win that daily battle is know-ing this: God was never meant to be fully understood by us. In John 14:21 (NLT), Jesus says "Those who accept my command-ments and obey them are the ones who love me." He doesn't say those who *understand* and obey, but those who *accept* and obey. God doesn't require complete understanding before we can say "yes" to him. In fact, he doesn't expect us to understand at all. He simply wants those who truly love him to do what he's asked—without delay or half-heartedness.

I want to be able to take the plunge willingly, fearlessly, enthu-siastically—like a kid who, after backing up to get a running start, launches himself into the pool for his first cannonball of summer. Why would I show up any less excited? I know God isn't going to abandon me in my obedience. Have I forgotten that even having the ability to obey God is a privilege? The wind and waves obey him (Mark 4:41), but they don't have the option to choose other-wise. We can't forget that the greatest honor of our earthly—and eternal—lives is to have the choice and to choose well.

The good news about obedience? We're actually told that the more we obey, the more we'll understand. "To those who listen to my teaching, more understanding will be given. But for those who are not listening, even what little understanding they have will be taken away from them" (Mark 4:25 NLT). If you keep seek-ing God, if you continue to hear his commands, you'll become wiser, and obedience will become easier (though not necessarily in that order). We were never promised the full picture—just a little more of it.

Obedience before Satisfaction

According to Maslow's hierarchy of needs, "self-actualization" is one of the most critical human needs and, when met, results in "happiness, peace of mind, and satisfaction."[4] In other words, it's the pursuit of your ideal self, your hopes, your ambitions. While I understand the theory behind this pyramid—humans have physiological and psychological needs—I also recognize that if you're a follower of Christ, most of the needs described here aren't really needs at all, but secular hopes. In addition to food, water, and air (duh), the list also suggests that independence, social prestige, and financial security are all needs that we must work to meet. Isn't this starting to sound like the American dream? Well, sister, that's no coincidence.

I've said it before (quite a few times) and I'll say it again— Jesus didn't come so we could enjoy brunch with a view or live in fancy homes. He didn't come so we could be rich and satisfied. But because of the American dream, because of decades-old psychological theories, we've been taught to think that even though he made the ultimate sacrifice to save us, the point of our purpose here is still to chase power, possessions, and pleasure. Because after all, these are basic needs, right?

Even before worrying about food and water, which *are* fundamental human needs, Jesus told his followers to "seek first the kingdom of God" (Matt. 6:33 CSB). The rest is up to God, and he promises as much.

- "My God will supply all your needs according to *his* riches" (Phil. 4:19 CSB—emphasis mine).
- "And we know that for those who love God all things work together for good, for those who are called according to *his* purpose" (Rom. 8:28 ESV—emphasis mine).
- "He accomplishes infinitely more than we might ask or think" (Eph. 3:20 NLT)—according to *his* power at work within us.

We must reevaluate our needs so we no longer run the risk of thinking that what he's given isn't good enough. We must stop pretending that we deserve what the world tells us we do—new, nicer. We must acknowledge, before it's too late, that we were never meant to live in a space of satisfaction outside the heart of God because worldly desires really do "wage war against the soul" (1 Pet. 2:11 AMP).

The American dream tells us we must play by its rules to experience satisfaction and happiness; Jesus tells us we must surrender our hearts and satisfaction will come—a sense of fulfillment the Bible refers to as joy, gladness not based on circumstance (1 Pet. 1:8–9). While happiness is a fleeting, outward expression to be pursued, joy is given by the Lord (Eccles. 2:26) and must simply be accepted. It is said to be "the spontaneous result of being filled with the holy spirit."[5]

Unfortunately for us, we're a bit mixed-up. Happiness and joy are not interchangeable. We assume weekend hobbies and lifelong friendships can provide joy, when, in reality, they only have the power to offer happiness. This assumption is a danger to our well-being. Take a second and think about what makes you happy. Is it a current project at work or the flowers blooming in your garden? Maybe it's the blueberry lemon loaf you just pulled from the oven or the way your six-year-old smiles when she sees you in the carpool line. While these things seem precious and fulfilling, they are also things that fade away. Happiness is like that; it comes and goes. Joy, on the other hand, is not only precious and fulfilling, it endures to eternity.

Even still, people will argue that God wants us to be happy. These are the same people who assume if we lay at his feet all the things that make us happy, we will inevitably lose our happiness, too. But maybe that's the point. Happiness, the way we experience it, is a lie; it's a fallible human emotion that Satan uses to dress up our lives, to keep us in a space of satisfaction. In fact, the historical definition of *happy* is "lucky, favored by fortune"—from the root word *hap*, which means *chance*.[6] And sister friend, you haven't received a single thing from the Lord by chance. He is intentional and generous and wants us to experience more than a fleeting sense of happiness—he wants us to know joy.

While talking to his disciples in the upper room, Jesus said, "I have told you these things so that you will be filled with my joy. Yes, your joy will overflow!" (John 15:11 NLT). And what are these "things" Jesus referred to? They are obedience and prayer—the essentials of remaining in him. Happiness is the result of serving yourself. Joy is the result of serving your Savior. "How joyful are those who fear the LORD and delight in obeying his commands" (Ps. 112:1 NLT).

Nevertheless, it will take every ounce of your being to give up what you want so God may be glorified. It will require an incredible amount of self-discipline to stop yourself from reaching for comfort and instead take hold of obedience. Maybe try it, just once. Deny yourself and take up your cross to simply experience what it feels like. We can do hard things when we really want to, especially with and for the Lord. We can choose to be obedient before we understand. We can choose to be obedient before we're satisfied.

Below, I've listed two things that hinder my faith walk: lack of understanding and the pursuit of satisfaction. I left a blank space for you to add your own—just becoming aware of what they are is a huge step toward surrendering them to God. My prayer is that we can let go of these and move forward with hearts that ache to be obedient.

I choose obedience before_____understanding_____.

I choose obedience before_____satisfaction_____.

I choose obedience before_____.

Prayer

Father, teach me to be blindly obedient. Turn my heart back to you and make me brave. Allow me to experience the fruit of obedience, the blessing of your presence—a fullness of joy. Please remind me that this type of contentment can't be found anywhere else. Thank you for giving me countless chances to walk in servility.

NOTES

[1] David Guzik, "Study Guide for Exodus 20: The Ten Commandments," Blue Letter Bible, June 2022, https://www.blueletterbible.org/comm/guzik_david/study-guide/exodus/exodus-20.cfm.

[2] Ralph G. Nichols, quoted in Carol Bradford, "The Power of Listening," Ohio State University College of Medicine, November 2020, https://medicine.osu.edu/ohio-state-medicine-dr-bradford-message/november-2020#:~:text=Ralph%20G.,is%20to%20listen%20to%20them.

[3] Dictionary.com, s.v. "faith" (*n.*), accessed July 3, 2024, https://www.dictionary.com/browse/faith.

[4] "Maslow's Hierarchy of Needs," *Harappa* (blog), March 3, 2021, https://harappa.education/harappa-diaries/maslows-hierarchy-of-needs/#heading_3.

[5] Paul A. Crow et al., "Joy in Human Existence," *Encyclopedia Britannica*, last updated May 7, 2024, https://www.britannica.com/topic/Christianity/Joy-in-human-existence.

[6] *Online Etymology Dictionary*, s.v. "happiness" (*n.*), accessed June 11, 2024, https://www.etymonline.com/word/happiness.

NINE

Goals, Guidance, and a *Good God*

Although Jesus was the sinless son of God, we don't look at his life often enough and wish for something similar. Why? Because, to us, there's nothing obvious worth wanting. He didn't win a Nobel Peace Prize. He didn't sign a fifty-million-dollar contract with the NFL. He didn't own Facebook or have his own reality TV show. In fact, from the very start, we are told of humble beginnings.

While everything in the Old Testament foreshadowed the arrival of a messianic king, the world largely failed to recognize Jesus when he stepped out of heaven and into a stable one silent, holy night. He wasn't born into a prominent family but to parents who were surrounded by scandal. He wasn't delivered in a top hospital or in the comfort or privacy of his family's own home. Instead, God thought a horse stall would be a more appropriate setting for the start of our saving story. Although Jesus's arrival was less than glamorous, it was nothing short of miraculous.

It's clear to us that Jesus was created for a purpose, and never once in his thirty-three years did he step outside the lines of it. (That's something worth wanting!) He never wavered in his beliefs or became distracted or uninterested. He didn't work full time to make ends meet and then do ministry when and how he could. He lived and breathed for the purposes of God and everything else came after—what to eat, what to wear, where to stay, and for how long. The Bible never mentions Jesus's home, his clothes, hair, or physique. None of it matters in his story, and when we get to heaven, we'll realize it also doesn't matter in ours. The only reason these things matter to us right now is because society tells us they should. The American dream is self-centered, hard-working, materialistic. Jesus would most likely be considered a failure among us. He would be viewed as a loser, a misfit, definitely not someone you'd want your daughter to marry. I can hear it now: "He doesn't have a job, a car, or a credit score!"

I've noticed that, unfortunately, the more successful we are in the eyes of the world, the more we look at people who unreservedly follow God *instead* of the American dream and think, "They ain't got a clue." Maybe we look at their lifestyle and assume they've failed themselves and their families because they don't have their lives planned out like we do. Maybe we unintentionally judge them because their priorities don't look like ours. Or, perhaps deep down, we feel sorry for them because they'll never be able to afford what we can. When our mindset is this small, this secular, it keeps us from realizing, even as Christians, that a life lived for Jesus only happens when a life is lived *like* Jesus (1 John 2:6). In one of his last prayers before the crucifixion, Jesus told the Father: "I brought glory to you here on earth by completing the work you gave me to do" (John 17:4 NLT). Don't you want to be able to say the same thing to God at the end of your life and be right? Oh, to be like Jesus—the ultimate example.

How to Be Like Jesus in Loving and Serving the Lord

His Prayers and Purpose | My mother-in-law had an illustrious career in federal law enforcement. Although she's retired now, I often wonder how many times, if ever, in the thirty-two years she spent in her male-dominated field, she had to step out of a room to remind herself that she belonged there. Did her colleagues ever suggest otherwise? I also wonder if women in the military have to do this. Or women who work in construction. Or even women who work in the church. The world is constantly suggesting that we don't belong in the places we find ourselves, and to a large extent, the world is right.

A few days ago, I reacted poorly to something that, in the grand scheme of things, didn't matter. I let my emotions get the best of me and immediately regretted my choice of words. I locked myself in the bathroom to cry, and when the tears finally stopped, I looked at myself in the mirror. I stared into my own eyes for what felt like forever, and after a few quiet moments of self-reflection, I told the woman looking back at me, "You don't belong here. Start acting like it." I'd never considered myself to be a chameleon, easily influenced by my surroundings. Yet there I was, operating in a worldly fashion, not the manner in which I should've been acting as a child of God, a citizen of heaven. I need to be more like Jesus, who never once forgot where he came from or where he was going (John 13:3). He not only claimed to be the Son of God, but his actions and reactions suggested it was true.

Jesus didn't do anything of his own accord. He lived for the purposes of the Father. "For I have come down from heaven to do the will of God who sent me, not to do my own will" (John 6:38 NLT). As a follower of Christ, I should be more interested in his will than

I am my own, but obviously this isn't always the case. Nor am I fully reliant on the Father. Jesus even said, "the Son can do nothing by himself" (John 5:19 NLT), and if Jesus can't operate solo, then how lost must I be to assume I can manage on my own? Why would I even want to? Jesus depended on the Father to not only provide physical and spiritual nourishment, but to provide the framework for his earthly ministry. To Jesus, it didn't feel like rocket science—he simply imitated the work and will of God. "Whatever the Father does, the Son also does" (John 5:19 NLT). This, too, is our mission.

For us to step into this, however, we must seek God's presence as Jesus did. While he ministered in a constant state of travel, he, without exception, took time to dwell unaccompanied in the presence of God. In the wilderness, in the garden, up the mountain, all night, in isolated places, Jesus prayed. He shows us, by example, that silence and solitude are our way back to the source. When was the last time you made a sacred space for God? Stood in his presence, on holy ground? I'm sure your soul is thirsty for another drink, and he is the only thing that will ever truly satisfy it.

How to Be Like Jesus in Loving and Serving Others

His Acceptance and Generosity | If we learn to love and serve the Lord the way Jesus did, we'll eventually learn to love and serve his people the right way, too. Jesus chose to take the position of a slave, declaring that he came "not to be served but to serve" (Matt. 20:28 NLT). How many of us exhibit this attitude when we're getting our car valeted or having someone else carry our bags? We live to please ourselves, and this brings a sense of entitlement that isn't from the Lord. The creator of the universe? The author of life? He never acted entitled, though by definition, he *was* entitled and extremely deserving of privileges, special treatment, recognition, and honor. But this isn't what he sought. Instead, he sought the salvation and welfare of others.

The only one who has the authority to judge humankind at the end of it all chose to walk the Earth without being judgmental. He didn't come to criticize anyone's appearance or make fun of their life choices. He came to "seek and save those who are lost" (Luke 19:10 NLT). As followers of Christ, we have an obligation to reach out and rescue. Yet, we often forget that we're the ones responsible *now* for what Jesus did then. Only God can do the rescuing, but we do him no favors by trying to decide if the person he's placed in front of us is worthy of our time or friendship. What we may really be trying to decide is whether or not we think they're worthy of salvation.

One of my neighbors was telling me about a friend she wanted me to meet. "She's kind of overweight, but she's great," is the only part of the story I remember now. This is the epitome of our culture, and it bleeds over into our faith walk. We only want to be seen with our skinny friends. Our "dream" guys are always wealthy. We don't want homeless people attending our church. We care who we're seen with and with whom we're associated, and this closes off the kingdom of God. It makes it seem like a gated community where only certain people are welcome—a place where, without a parking pass, "violators will be towed."

In the 2008 recession, my father lost his job, along with three million other Americans. Without hesitation, he went to work stocking shelves at a local grocery store. While I was too young to fully understand the gravity of the situation, I was able to notice the toll it took on his self-esteem. The concept of the American dream hadn't served him well in that moment. Our culture, even among Christians, didn't commend him for doing what it took to provide for his family. Instead, it told him that he was a poor provider, a worthless father, a failure. He was embarrassed because society told him he should be. He wasn't able to see, and was never lovingly reminded, that the experience hadn't changed his worth to the Lord, his place in God's kingdom, or his home in eternity.

Jesus didn't make mistakes. Nor did he decide if someone was worthy of salvation based on their physical appearance or job title. So, what gives us the authority to refuse acceptance, to look down on a set of circumstances? The recipients of Paul's letters said this of him: "Paul's letters are demanding and forceful, but in person he is weak, and his speeches are worthless" (2 Cor. 10:10 NLT)! Leave it to us to take one of the most powerful redemption stories in Scripture and reduce it to the individual's physical appearance. History has been too busy discussing Paul's unibrow[1] to remember that God used him in ways we could only dream about. Originally a killer of Christians, Paul encountered the Lord on the way to Damascus. The Lord physically blinded Paul so that he might eventually see the truth—and he did. Paul spent the rest of his life spreading the gospel until he, himself, was killed for his faith.

We must stop assuming we're better, more valuable, than we really are just because the world tells us that our background, our family structure, our finances are "better" than that of someone else. This not only diminishes the reality of our own faults, but it keeps us from loving others the way Jesus did. In the Gospel accounts, Jesus is portrayed as a "friend of tax collectors and other sinners" (Matt. 11:19; Luke 7:34 NLT). We quote these scriptures but wouldn't be at ease among prostitutes or prisoners. We don't look at them through the eyes of Jesus but through the eyes of the judicial system. Do we assume that we ourselves aren't sinners or that our own sins are not as serious?

In John 8:7, when the crowd told Jesus that the adulterous woman among them deserved to be killed, he said, "All right, but let the one who has never sinned throw the first stone" (NLT)! The men in the crowd snuck away after realizing they couldn't condemn her sin because they themselves weren't sinless. In the Sermon on the Mount, Jesus also declares, "The standard you use in judging is the standard by which you will be judged" (Matt. 7:2 NLT). Is this not enough for us? Scott Hubbard, the pastor of All Peoples Church in Minneapolis, asks, "How many emails would be abandoned and text messages unsent, how many thoughts would be discarded, and words unsaid, how many conversations would be redirected, if only we heard our Savior say, with eternal sobriety in his voice, 'Judge not'?"[2] We're called, rather, to assess the fruit that other people's lives produce (John 7:24), and we're asked to do it wisely, properly, and in a way that honors God.

Jesus graciously accepted promiscuous women, greedy men, and everyone in between, but that doesn't mean he approved of their lifestyle or the condition of their heart. Yet, even still, he gave freely—compassion (Luke 7:11–17), forgiveness (Luke 23:34), even his own life (Rom. 5:8). He put the needs of others before his own (Mark 6:30–44), exemplifying profound generosity. I want my children to look at my life and know that Jesus and his people far outclass material things. I want them to understand the generosity of Jesus because they see my own.

On numerous occasions growing up, I witnessed my dad blessing others because of how much he appreciated his own blessings. Less than a year after Hurricane Katrina made landfall in South Louisiana, we were sitting in a restaurant in New Orleans. Our waitress came to take our drink order, and instead of just exchanging pleasantries, my dad asked her how she was *really* doing.

Her eyes filled with tears, but in trying to keep the situation pleasant, she minimized the aftermath by saying she was "just trying to keep the lights on for her kids." My dad, after paying the bill, literally ran out of the restaurant and down the street. It didn't make sense in my ten-year-old mind until she came out after him, crying and screaming. While I never asked him how much cash he left at the table, it was clearly enough to give her some sort of hope. He hadn't stopped to consider how worthy she was or wasn't. He hadn't wondered if she was telling the truth. He quietly erred on the side of compassion and chose to give freely.

One foggy morning on his commute across Lake Pontchartrain, my dad watched as the car in front of him broke through the concrete barrier and plunged into the water. Although there wasn't a safe place to pull over, he chose to stop anyway. When he saw the driver reach the surface of the water, he threw him the life jacket that had been in the backseat of our car. He didn't stay at the scene but was mentioned in the following day's paper as the onlooker who saved the driver's life. What if my dad had stopped to consider whether or not the person was worth the life preserver? Doesn't that seem absurd? Well, it is, and it would be just as delusional to stop and wonder if the person God placed in our life is worth a lifeline, the good news of the gospel. Our job, simply put, is to give freely.

How to Be Like Jesus in Dealing with the (Girl) Stuff

His Deep, Human Emotion | Let's get out of our own way. For me, that means learning to control my emotions. Jesus didn't tell a single person to follow their heart. He told them to give up their lives, take up their cross, "and follow" him (Matt. 16:24 NLT). Jesus never encouraged anyone to live their truth. He told them that he was "the way, the truth, and the life" (John 14:6 NLT). Jesus never told anyone to believe in themselves. He told them to "believe in God; believe also in me" (John 14:1 CSB). We'll never be like Jesus if we continue to let our emotions manipulate us.

I'm rude to people when I let my feelings get the best of me. I worry about things after my distorted thoughts tell me I should.

I impulse buy when I allow my mood to dictate my stewardship—and there's no way to justify these behaviors. They won't ever be pleasing or glorifying to God. It's clear that, as a human, Jesus felt deep emotion, just as we do. Yet, he was not only able to control them, but he also never sinned because of them. In Mark 3:5, the religious leaders chose to reject Jesus, even after watching him heal a man on the Sabbath. This is one of the few places where Jesus's emotions are mentioned in the synoptic Gospels. Yet, even in his anger, he didn't cuss them out or cut them down. We're told that, instead, "He looked around them angrily and was deeply saddened by their hard hearts" (Mark 3:5 NLT). He was angry but did not sin because of it (Eph. 4:26).

You know when people say something mean about someone else but justify it by also saying, "I'd even say it to their face?" This usually doesn't happen when the presence of God is also being thought about. If we're called to be "taking every thought captive to the obedience of Christ" (2 Cor. 10:5 LEB), then we should be examining every single thing that crosses our mind—not merely what we want to say out loud, but every thought we ever have. Perhaps then, we might not be so bold in the words and thoughts we have that aren't glorifying to the Lord.

In Luke 19, we read that when Jesus came closer to Jerusalem and saw the city, "he began to weep" (Luke 19:41 NLT). They had ultimately rejected his teachings and would be attacked by the Roman empire. He experienced frustration and grief and anger, the same way we do. His human heart had the ability to break. Yet he didn't become closed off. The Bible itself is a book of stories where people group after people group trust and then turn from the Lord. He never becomes calloused to this but continues to accept others and freely give.

Prayer

Father, God, help me to recognize you in the midst of everything else that vies for my attention. Help me sort through the "stuff" so I can find and focus on what truly matters to heaven. Make me more like you, Jesus, in the way I seek the Father, love other people, and respond to the world beyond myself. I want to be fully reliant on you, not myself, and live for your purposes, not my own.

NOTES

[1] Abraham J. Malherbe, "A Physical Description of Paul," *Harvard Theological Review* 79, no. 1–3 (1986): 170–75. https://doi.org/10.1017/S0017816000020435.

[2] Scott Hubbard, "Judge Others as You Want to Be Judged," *desiringGod*, September 9, 2021, https://www.desiringgod.org/articles/judge-others-as-you-want-to-be-judged.

TEN

In Him, You Are Brave

It was a rainy Sunday morning in East Africa. Months earlier, I had volunteered to speak on the topic of silence and solitude in front of a small Kenyan congregation. I was a naïve sixteen-year-old who hated public speaking. In fact, I disliked it so much that I refused to think about it or prepare for it until panic began to set in only a few days earlier. As I sat there and listened to opening remarks, I remember feeling unconnected and overwhelmed. One of my team members, sensing my dread, leaned over and whispered a phrase so plain, yet so powerful. Little did I know, its truth would echo through the hallways of my life even years later. "In him, you are brave."

My heart scooped up these words, and almost immediately, I felt the anxiety drain from my body. In that moment, I was able to take a deep breath and acknowledge God and his sovereignty. *Okay, God. It's you and me.* While I can't recall what I said at the podium, I do remember the pivotal moment that changed the course of where I was heading. God had brought me through something as simple as public speaking to remind me that I can be brave in the shadow of his wings (Ps. 91:4).

When I was pregnant with Riley, I became deeply fearful of giving birth—the pain, the vulnerability, the uncertainty of what I was about to endure. Even the recovery process seemed to scare me. Before I knew it, my water had broken, and I was sitting in an empty emergency room in the middle of the night. Carson had gone to park the car, and the nurses had settled me in and were back at their station. The room was unwelcoming and cold. I felt a rush of fear, an emotion I had expected but a type I had never experienced. In the silence, I spoke out to Jesus. I laid my life at his feet. *Okay, God. It's you and me.* And just like at the small Kenyan church years before, I was physically able to feel the anxiety flow out through my hands. My heart welled with a sense of peace that could've only come from heaven. I spent eight hours, comfortably, in labor and delivered Riley within an hour of my (favorite) doctor arriving. As they placed Riley on my chest, all bundled, I couldn't help but cry. Not only because I felt I recognized him; not only because a new, precious heartbeat was meeting mine for the first time; but because God had brought me through the hardest part. He had made me brave.

We were down to the last few minutes before Carson had to board the plane. Our first deployment. Heavy, hard, emotions surged through my fingertips. I was distraught, but in a very put together, quiet, normal way. As I stood there in the parking lot and watched him walk away—our one-year-old in the backseat of my car—I spoke through my tears into the silence. *Okay, God. It's you and me.* My broken heart wasn't mended in that moment, but for those six months, he made me brave.

When I was writing this book, I learned early in the process that although I don't have all the answers, I know what needs to be done to ditch the American dream, forever. I know how to let go of things that aren't pointing me to Jesus. But am I willing to do so? Do I have what it takes? Or will I end up being what many people call us Christians—a hypocrite? One night, I sat at my computer for what seemed like forever and watched the cursor blink. *Okay, God. It's you and me.* I acknowledged my sin and shortcomings, and I asked God to make me brave. And if this book ever gets to sit on a shelf somewhere, I guess he did.

When everything is stripped away and you're in an unknown place, alone and empty-handed, it really is just you and God, your spirit settling into the one that is holy. Although sometimes this space makes us feel like we're on autopilot or in hyperdrive, we were meant to live this close to Jesus. This is holy ground, the dust we came from. But it feels so foreign because we seldom find ourselves here. We decorate and renovate our lives and our minds until we forget that our hands were ever empty. We add throw pillows and scented candles and layers upon layers of distractions. And we forget that he is essential to our very existence.

The deepest part of my heart is repulsed by the thought of having a comfortable, picture-perfect life. It never concerns itself with wealth, beauty, or popularity. It craves a space where the work of Jesus is being done boldly and sacrificially—a space that is holy. It urges me to abandon my current life and comforts, lay them at the feet of Jesus, and walk (no, run!) faithfully toward whatever it is he has for me. Nothing else matters but careful obedience. The shallowest part of my heart, however, and the part most easily accessible, longs for what is earthly. I want Botox and a boob job. A personal trainer and a European vacation. A Volvo. I want my nails done and my teeth whitened and for someone else to clean my house. When I'm lingering at the edge of materialism and I'm seeking more, when my heart just wants to enjoy life and take the easy route, the path that is wide, that's when I ask God to shift my focus from myself to *me plus Jesus*—and he does. He makes me brave enough to live where I was meant to. And he can make you brave, too.

You Can Be Brave Because He's with You Always

"And be sure of this: I am with you always, even to the end of the age" (Matt. 28:20 NLT). When Jesus sent his disciples to the ends of the Earth, he also sent with them his spirit. We can trust that the Holy Spirit is with us, too, and we can be brave knowing he offers power, protection, patience, and, ultimately, paradise.

You Can Be Brave Because He Won't Fail You, Ever

First Chronicles 28:20 (NLT) says, "Be strong and courageous, and do the work. Don't be afraid or discouraged, for the LORD God, my God, is with you. He will not fail you or forsake you." In this passage, David is encouraging his son, Solomon, not only to be brave, but to be brave *and do*. David had originally planned to build God's temple, but after acts of war disqualified him from doing so, the Lord chose Solomon in his place. David is suggesting here that we can't sit around and dream about a life well lived for Jesus—we must get up and do the work. While we might be afraid to take the first step, we know that the Lord won't ever let us down or leave us. This alone should make us brave, just as it made Solomon, who completed the temple seven years later.

You Can Be Brave Because
He Values You More Than Anything

"And the very hairs on your head are all numbered. So don't be afraid; you are more valuable to God than a whole flock of sparrows" (Luke 12:7 NLT). The Bible tells us that because we're made in God's image, set apart from the rest of creation, we have no reason to be afraid of anything. If he cares about the number of hair follicles on your scalp, I bet he also cares about walking you through whatever it is you're worried about.

You Can Be Brave Because
He Commands You to Be

When the Lord was preparing the way to the promised land after Moses's death, he told Joshua, "Have I not commanded you? Be strong and courageous! . . . for the LORD your God is with you wherever you go" (Josh. 1:9 AMP). Joshua knew, after Moses had shared God's plan regarding Canaan, that he would be the one to successfully lead the Israelites. Yet, even with a promised victory, God still commanded him to be brave. The same is true for us. We, too, have a promised victory, a promised land, and God is commanding us to be brave on our journey toward it.

You Can Be Brave Because
He Makes You So

"For God has not given us a spirit of fear and timidity, but of power, love, and self-discipline" (2 Tim. 1:7 NLT).

Paul was speaking to Timothy in this instance about how fear isn't an emotion we receive from the Lord. It isn't a trait inherited from heaven, and if he didn't create the human spirit to be fearful, frightened, or afraid, he must have made it to be brave.

To some of you, this concept may seem a bit rudimentary. But if you're someone who struggles with materialism—if you're a Christian who continues to choose the American dream—then bravery is what you're going to need to be able to walk forward in faithfulness. It won't be easy to change your lifestyle. It won't be fun to turn left when everyone else is going right, it won't be painless to deny yourself daily, but being brave for the purposes of God will bring you back to holy ground—the presence of God (Exod. 3:5) and the pursuit of the new Jerusalem (Rev. 21:2).

What We Can Do with the Bravery He Gives

He'll make you brave enough to let go of dreams that once felt so big and meaningful but were never his to begin with. The world is pushy. It tries to confirm things God hasn't ordained or spoken into. I had never dreamed about working in higher education, but a year after college, I found myself in a graduate program that was propelling me into a career in college admissions. People in my proximity told me that I was "living the dream," and for a while, I believed them. I should've known that sometimes when everything seems perfect, it's not God confirming your path but Satan encouraging your complacency.

I would still be working at a university if God hadn't shut so many doors in my face. I would also venture to say that he had to close the windows, transoms, and floor vents, too. (Apparently,

I'm a slow learner). Of course, he closed each one lovingly and patiently, but it still always felt abrupt, offensive, and embarrassing. In hindsight, it's easy for me to recognize that I wasn't in the right place, but in the moment, I was too busy to notice.

Even when selecting a college major, I wasn't seeking his will for my life. I was checking a box, under pressure. We do this, as Americans, in every aspect of our lives. We want to be successful, and even when we're told it's a "grind," we don't flinch. We get on the path toward prosperity, and we never stop running. We don't make time to seek his kingdom, to walk in obedience. We don't make time for holy ambitions. As Christians, we know better than to live this way. We shouldn't *want* to live this way. Jesus says that his "yoke is easy," and his "burden is light" (Matt. 11:30 AMP); that success, with him, means resting in his presence and relying on his sovereignty. But once we've started running toward earthly success, once we've committed to the American dream, it's hard to see things for what they are, and it's hard to be brave in extracting ourselves from them.

If your hands are holding this book, I've been praying for you. I've repeatedly asked God to capture your attention long enough to start a chain of events that ultimately brings you to a place of careful obedience. For this to happen, I've also asked God, on your behalf, for bravery. Chances are, you're already living a well-established life, and if you're just now seeking his kingdom or his dreams for you, then I'm praying that you'll be flexible enough to make some difficult but necessary changes. You might have to sell your possessions and move overseas, or maybe not. You might have to quit your job and start over, even with three kids at home. Or maybe not. There are a million places God could take you, and trust me, sister friend, every single one of them is better than the dream you've built for yourself. You'll just have to be brave enough to lay your own desires at the feet of Jesus and, in their place, pick up what he has for you. I can't champion you toward this enough. I feel like your biggest cheerleader—with so much hype, so much adrenaline—yelling from the sidelines. "Keep going!" "Do the hard things!" "You were meant for this!"

When I quit my job a few years ago, people just assumed I was trading corporate America for the life of a stay-at-home mom. While they aren't totally wrong, God had additional plans for the rearranging, the slowing down, of my everyday life. While Riley slept beside me, I started writing this book. I told all of four people that, maybe one day, "ten years from now," I'll try and get it published. It was a God-given dream but still a dream that initially seemed so unattainable, so impractical, to not only me but to several others who decided to voice their opinions. Yet, it's the only dream of mine that has ever really worked. I probably would've laughed (and then thrown up) if you had told me ten years ago that I'd be writing books. But I'm only in this position because I decided to fully surrender my heart to God, and in turn, he made me brave. He commanded me to be so. I can't remember a dream I've had for myself that has been crazier or larger or less possible than the dream I'm currently living. Thank you, Jesus, for making me brave.

He'll make you brave enough to be who he created you to be. Has anyone ever told you that Jesus's opinion is the only one that matters? While I do believe this to be both factual and reassuring, I've never been able to completely let go of what the world thinks too. Society tells us we should want to retire a millionaire, we should want to be size two, we should want an invitation to the Junior League. And if you do want these things, well, me too, sister! We all want to feel financially secure, well-liked, and invited in. But the standard, the expectation, is so harsh—often so unreasonable—that ultimately, we're striving for something we'll never reach, something we weren't designed to reach.

I've always been too worried about the opinions of other people to realize it doesn't matter what they think or even what we ourselves think—it matters what Jesus thinks. And he doesn't think we need to be quadruple billionaires, runway models, or sophisticated housewives. He thinks we need to be what we were created to be—bearers of his image.

God, make us brave(r). We can't, on our own, let go of things that have continually provided us a sense of security—however fleeting they may be. Our culture has taught us to need things that aren't necessary, to define ourselves by them. Because of this, handing our comfortable retirement back to God isn't going to be stress free. Laying our self-interests at his feet won't be a cakewalk. It will require of us major life changes, incredible mental and spiritual shifts. But regardless of how hard it seems at first, he isn't going to abandon us in our obedience. He'll carry us the whole way if our hearts remain willing.

He'll make you brave enough to step out in faith, regardless of what your family and friends might think or what they're doing with their own lives. I hope you've surrounded yourself with people who truly love the Lord and who will support you and champion you in your bravery. I do recognize, however, that this isn't always the case. Sometimes when you choose to get up and do the work—when you intentionally start propelling yourself in the direction of Christ—it has a devastating impact on relationships. You might strain your marriage. You might lose some friends. In the thick of it, remember that only his opinion matters, he commanded you to be brave, and his plans never miss a detail or exclude a person. Although it might be awkward at times and certainly difficult, you can find rest knowing that someone, somewhere, even maybe someone in the periphery of your life, will notice your heart change, your bravery, and maybe they'll want to know more about this God of yours.

As I mentioned earlier, Christians (particularly female Christians) are often labeled as irrelevant, outdated, and unaccepting. Instead of emboldening us, this can crush us before we even have a chance to stand. When I was able to fully grasp that this was the way the world perceived me, I let it mess with my head. I didn't cling to God's opinion or allow him to make me brave. In situations where I should've stepped out in faith, I didn't step out at all. I was afraid people wouldn't take me seriously or I'd come across the wrong way and do more damage than good. Yet, Christians around the world, specifically in Africa and the Middle East, are being killed for their faith. Horrifically tortured, brutally murdered. While all I really worry about is being made fun of, insulted, or unfriended. These things are minor in comparison, but they still require a level of bravery to withstand. And if he's making people brave enough to share the gospel in India, he has the ability to make us brave enough to live like a friend of Christ wherever we are. When the world starts hating us because we're affiliated with Jesus, we can be brave knowing it hated him first (John 15:18–19).

He'll make you brave enough to start using your resources in a new and wild way. It is sometimes said that "God's blessings are not in what he gives, but what he takes away." Just another quote we hang on our walls but don't truly comprehend or ache to experience. We like to think that we'll rejoice unhesitatingly in any situation, but when good things are taken from us, we struggle immensely. At times, his blessings look like healthy children, a steady job, extra money, four walls and a roof. Other times, they look like a hospital stay, a job loss, an eviction. An alteration of our hearts and minds; an opportunity to step back, step down, slow down, simplify. An undoing that takes us back to a place where we can restart—where his blessings are noted, acknowledged, and accepted with gratitude and awe. A place where our hearts overflow instead of overlook.

A few years ago, I stopped getting my nails done in a salon. I felt too guilty about spending over a hundred dollars a month on something so frivolous. After all, it's God's money anyway, right? At first, I was bummed because I no longer felt pretty or put together. As shallow as it sounds, I really had to wrestle with the decision and remind myself that obedient is what I wanted to be—even before I wanted to be pretty or put together. Eventually, though, it became a blessing. We had extra money to give back to God. Not just the ability to tithe but the ability to offer. This makes me wonder what else we can give up so God can use even more of our resources for the things he originally intended.

Although we're always just a few steps away from losing everything, we tell ourselves we're secure and comfortable. Money, homes, possessions—they blind us to this reality. They lead us to believe we could never be homeless or in any kind of position to struggle. *We're blessed. We're highly favored.* We think our lifestyle is a blessing from God. But as I've already questioned, have you ever wondered if your lifestyle is actually a misuse of his blessing? We're too well-off in the United States to even imagine having, owning, or seeking less. Inevitably, rearranging our spending habits for God seems risky, especially when we have families to provide for and entertain; a lifestyle to maintain. But if your treasure is being stored where it's supposed to, shouldn't that be a sense of security in and of itself? In his book *You and Me Forever*, Francis Chan says, "people accuse me of going overboard preparing for my first ten million years in eternity; in my opinion, people go overboard in worrying about their last ten years on earth."[1] It may seem like your life here will always be "less than," but you can believe that your eternity will be so much more.

It takes bravery—and a lot of wise decision-making—to realize and accept that your human heart isn't going to get its way anymore. I jokingly tell my husband that "we only get one life to live, and I'll die without having ever owned a Volvo." It feels weird to deny myself something that was once so coveted. Yet wouldn't I rather die without having had a Volvo than die knowing I never truly lived for the Lord? While I imagine it must be nice to store up riches here on Earth, I imagine it's even nicer to enjoy the riches of heaven.

Does your lifestyle reflect your longing for heaven? Does the way you use your resources exemplify bravery and a devotion to Christ? Or does your life look like the epitome of the American dream? Psalms 84:10 (NLT) says, "A single day in your courts is better than a thousand anywhere else! I would rather be a gate-keeper in the house of my God than live the good life in the homes of the wicked." I want to jump up and emphatically agree with this, but my lifestyle would make an agreement seem hypocrit-ical. The word *wicked*, used here, according to Hebrew studies, doesn't necessarily mean evil but is used in a more subtle, mild, context to explain someone who appears righteous but doesn't serve the Lord.[2] Huh. That sounds like a casual Christian. That sounds like me.

We'd planned a weekend trip to Texas last summer, and when it didn't work out, I wasn't upset. I was shocked at my lack of emotion. Normally, I would be so down in the dumps, talking about how we never get to do anything fun and blah blah blah, totally discounting all that we *do* have and all that we get to do. But for the first time, I was okay with no vacation. My heart was content anyway. Why? Initially, I truly didn't know. But looking back now, I realize that instead of going on vacation, we bought the computer that essentially helped me write this book. God had made me brave enough to be okay with missing out *here* so I could store up treasure there. He had made me brave enough to lean into purpose before I leaned into pleasure. "Look! I am creating new heavens and a new earth, and no one will even think about the old ones anymore" (Isa. 65:17 NLT). While Texas vacations aren't a bad thing, they aren't an important thing, either. And, according to Scripture, when eternity meets us, we won't remember them anyway. The only thing that will be important is the holy ground we're standing on.

What It Means to Pursue Holiness

I hope you're feeling brave, friend. But, if you've made it here to the end of this book, you're probably feeling broken and burdened, too. When God first revealed to me the extent of my happiness, I refused to acknowledge it. He had moved me from spiritual blindness into a space that revealed a truth about my life that I wasn't yet ready to address. I told myself that while I could work on a few things—becoming less self-centered and less materialistic—I also didn't need to go overboard and change it all. Wasn't the stuff, the extra money, and the comfort a blessing from God anyway? Wasn't it an assurance that we were doing at least something right in his eyes? Wasn't it okay to source happiness from earthly satisfaction?

Even still, God continued to nudge me. Actually, it felt more like God was acting like a younger sibling—close to poking me but holding his finger a centimeter away and repeating over and over again, "I'm not touching you. I'm not touching you. I'm not touching you." I couldn't feel him, nor did I want to, but I knew he was there. One night, Carson and I finally confessed to each other what each of us had been wrestling with separately for weeks—we needed to offer God our whole lives, not just pieces of it, and that included his military career. People often look at me, as the spouse of a deployed servicemember, and say, "I don't know how you do it." While yes, the months of separation are hard, our time as a military family has been mostly wonderful. It has provided us with incredible health insurance and an income that some people never get to experience. It has allowed us to create the sort of pleasing and comfortable lifestyle that we originally thought we wanted and deserved.

God, for reasons not yet known, wanted to remind us that the lifestyle we were living isn't the kind he called us to. He allowed us to see that we've been guilty of trying to balance, albeit poorly, the American dream and his plan for our lives. Looking back on it, it does seem like maybe we were starting to get the two confused. When we found ourselves at a crossroads, we simply couldn't afford not to choose well. Laying Carson's career at the feet of Jesus would potentially mean giving up our health insurance, our income, and countless other benefits that had contributed to our complacency. It would mean stepping out in faith—for real this time—and letting God direct our steps. We have no secret safety nets or back up plans. God is all we have, but he's also all we need.

When I originally started this book, I worried about whether or not I would ever learn to walk this walk. But here I am, making the intentional decision to learn how to do so. I don't know what God has for us beyond the last bit of our military commitment, and the unknown scares me. Even so, we've made the decision to choose Jesus, to start over at square one, to rebuild on the right foundation. I pray that you'll do the same, no matter what it takes. It will seem unreal abandoning your current life, trying to get back to holy ground, back to Jesus, in hopes of starting over. The deepest part of my soul believes in his goodness, believes that he won't fail us—it's the rest of me that has to catch up.

Hebrews 10:14 (NIV) says, "By one sacrifice he has made perfect forever those who are being made holy." This is what keeps me grounded. This is what keeps my eyes on the prize. God promises here that we'll stand before him perfected and complete if we choose now, through faith, to let him make us holy. He's not saying we'll be considered faultless on account of a onetime decision to "follow" him; instead, it will be based on the ongoing process of sanctification.

The only thing I've ever known is the pursuit of happiness, but today and each day forward, I'm going to choose the pursuit of holiness. I'm sure it will end up being the hardest thing I've ever done, but I know that wherever the spirit of the Lord is, there's also freedom (2 Cor. 3:17). Freedom to let go, freedom to miss out, freedom to choose him and his ways and his purposes. And when we choose him, he'll choose us back. He chose us first. This should make us both brave and holy.

NOTES

[1]Francis Chan and Lisa Chan, *You and Me Forever: Marriage in Light of Eternity* (San Francisco: Claire Love, 2014).

[2]"Hebrew Word Study – The Wicked," *Chaim Bentorah*, May 7, 2018, https://www.chaimbentorah.com/2018/05/hebrew-word-study-the-wicked/.

Challenges

Hopefully, if these challenges don't totally align with your own struggles, they'll at least help you start thinking about steps you can take that will catapult you toward holiness, permanently. Simply being aware of your shortcomings, distractions, and sins will put you on a path to a faith that amazes Jesus.

Start a prayer journal. Four years ago, I decided to start using a sketch pad to fully write my prayers to God. It changed my faith. Massive prayers, colossal praises, endless hymns, lifesaving scriptures—for the first time, it was all neatly gathered in one place. Not one prayer, one thought, or one moment of thanksgiving was lost in hindsight. I was able to look back and see that even my forgotten prayers had been answered—what a Savior. This awareness made me more thankful for my relationship with Jesus, more astounded by his works, than I would've ever been without it. My brain doesn't have the capacity to see the big picture, but choosing to slow down and linger in his presence helped me to see a little bit more.

Admit your struggle. My husband doesn't care about material things; he never wants or buys "stuff"—yet here I was walking in the door with another designer bag, asking for a Volvo. When I finally came to terms with my materialism, I was too embarrassed to admit how "want-y" I'd become. But admitting your struggle isn't shameful; it's freeing. Chances are, your spouse or best friend, or whoever you confide in, already knows what you're battling because they know *you*. Bringing it out into the open, however, where you can be held accountable, will help your feet stay on the path of God; it will help your heart stay guarded. Jesus didn't care or even worry about material possessions, so he has the power to bring you into a space where you don't, either.

Go offline. If you're always looking to acquire more, if you constantly compare yourself to others, or if you're easily distracted by worldliness, anything you do online sure won't help. Not only are you getting advertisements for things you can't possibly need, but you're also watching everyone else spend their resources in ways that only serve themselves. Delete social media, cancel magazine subscriptions, and stop binge-watching TV. Whenever I have a free moment, whenever I want to relax or zone out, I scroll through endless posts on social media. It's just become a habit. But what if I had a habit of talking to God? Writing in my prayer journal? Meditating on Scripture? Telling others about Jesus?

Don't purchase impulsively. The next time you're out shopping and see something you want, don't buy it without thinking. Go home and consider if you really need it—most likely, you don't. Set aside the money anyway—as if you had spent it on what you wanted—and at the end of the week, month, year, whenever, use your savings for the purposes of God. This is a way to intentionally fight the desires of your flesh. I'm embarrassed that we're tripping over and tied down by the things we think we "need." Jesus traveled all over Israel with very little, but he was still able to complete the work God had given him.

Or don't purchase at all. If you know you're going to be too obsessed with an experience or possession, don't purchase it or participate in it. If it's something that your kids can ruin or other people can't borrow because it's too precious or too expensive, then you probably shouldn't have it anyway. Ask yourself this: Are you being a good steward of your resources if you acquire said item? Are you content with where your treasure is being stored? When Jesus returns, we won't have time to grab our diamonds or our Louis Vuitton bags, nor will we want to. So what's the point of allowing them to hinder a Christ-centered relationship with our kids or neighbors?

Remember, your things don't define you. Worldly goods are often used to measure a person's worth. As a result, we've become too concerned with what kind of car we drive, what neighborhood we live in, what college we did or did not attend, and not concerned enough about the impact we're making for the Lord. If we really do belong to God and if the purpose of life really is to bring him glory, then the brand of our tennis shoes matters very little, if at all. Our possessions don't define us, so if something we own makes us feel too entitled to remember this, then it probably needs to be put back where we found it.

Acknowledgments

Thank you, God, for making me brave, for proving that you use those whose hearts are willing.

Thank you to my husband, Carson. Your encouragement started this journey, and your steadiness in the midst of setbacks and unstable emotions kept me going. I couldn't have done this without your ridiculous positivity and rare form of selflessness. Thank you for pushing me toward this dream and being utterly unphased by the state of our messy, half-painted house. I will never *not* be crazy about you.

Thank you to my precious son, Riley. You changed my life three years ago, and I'll forever strive to love you well and walk you toward Jesus.

Thank you to my mother-in-law, Karen, for editing and re-editing every chapter of this book, who championed this calling and consistently sought God on my behalf. Thank you to her husband, my father-in-law, Craig, who sat in the playroom with Riley and ate lollipops so I could research, write, and pray.

Thank you to my precious parents who essentially dropped everything to support this endeavor. It seems as though everything in my life "takes a village," and I'll forever be grateful that you're such a large part of mine.

Thank you to my readers—my friends and sisters in Christ—who chose *not* to toss this book aside when things got ugly and uncomfortable. Let's continue to walk alongside each other in the pursuit of holiness so that one day we can stand before Jesus perfected and complete.

WHEN IT HURTS TO HOPE

RACHEL MILLER

Embrace the tension of unmet longing and choose hope—even when life doesn't look like you thought it would.

ISBN 978-1-68426-298-4

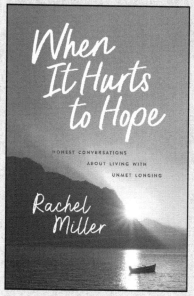

Maybe you've chosen to bury your dreams, denying your desires and sleepwalking through life. Maybe you've let your longing take the driver's seat and now you feel frantic and out of control. Even worse, you find yourself growing cold to God, wondering, *If I never get what I want, is God still good?* This book tackles that hard question—and many others.

When It Hurts to Hope will show you the middle ground between burying your longings and overindulging them. Rachel Miller offers encouragement and practical advice on how to honor God and honor your desires at the same time, sharing tools for being emotionally and spiritually healthy. Through storytelling, Scripture, and humor, this book will help you choose hope in tough seasons like unwanted singleness, infertility, chronic illness, and career frustrations. Ultimately, Jesus is the only one who can meet every longing.

1-877-816-4455 toll free
www.leafwoodpublishers.com

LEAFWOOD
PUBLISHERS
an imprint of Abilene Christian University Press

THE BURDEN OF BETTER

How a Comparison-Free Life Leads to Joy, Peace, and Rest

HEATHER CREEKMORE

ISBN 978-1-68426-470-4

Tired of chasing better?

In an era of carefully curated social media images, nonstop selfies, and TV shows devoted to perfection, comparison can consume you. Chasing something better quickly becomes a burden, weighing down your soul and preventing you from experiencing the freedom, contentment, and rest that God generously offers.

While other books on comparison call you to embrace your uniqueness, *The Burden of Better* reveals how only a deeper understanding of God's grace can guide you off the self-improvement treadmill. Heather's humor and empathetic approach offer a gospel-centered guide to kicking your comparison habit.

> "*The Burden of Better* is a refreshing drink of grace on a world-weary day. Trade your worries, fears, and addictions to comparison for the hope-filled truths Heather Creekmore mines for you. Read this book, and you'll experience the holy pause that can come at the end of perfectionism."
>
> **—Mary DeMuth,** author of *Pray Every Day: 90 Days of Prayer from God's Word*

1-877-816-4455 toll free
www.leafwoodpublishers.com

LEAFWOOD
P U B L I S H E R S
an imprint of Abilene Christian University Press